Waiting
A Bible Study
on Patience,
Hope, and Trust

Sharla Fritz

CONCORDIA PUBLISHING HOUSE · SAINT LOUIS

Published 2017 Concordia Publishing House
3558 S. Jefferson Avenue, St. Louis, MO 63118–3968
1-800-325-3040 • cph.org

Manufactured in the United States of America

1 2 3 4 5 6 7 8 9 10   26 25 24 23 22 21 20 19 18 17

Dedication

To my mother, Lorna,
who has inspired me with her love for the Savior.

Other Books by Sharla Fritz

Divine Design: 40 Days of Spiritual Makeover
Bless These Lips: 40 Days of Spiritual Renewal
Divine Makeover: God Makes You Beautiful
Soul Spa: 40 Days of Spiritual Renewal

Table of Contents

INTRODUCTION

We've all experienced the frustration of waiting. Waiting in bumper-to-bumper traffic. Waiting through airport security. Waiting for service in a restaurant.

Waiting to hear, "You've got the job!" Waiting for wedding bells. Waiting for test results. Waiting to be reconciled with a loved one.

And we despise it. In our modern culture of instant everything—same-day shipping, streaming movies, online banking, microwaveable meals—we are accustomed to getting everything we want *now*. So when our lives are put in a holding pattern, we complain and grumble and do anything we can to get things moving again.

But what if the waiting rooms of life are actually God's best classrooms? What if the Holy Spirit changes us through the uncomfortable delays of life? What if, in the waiting, the Lord draws us near and imparts lessons we could miss when our lives are flying at the speed of a Boeing 777?

Throughout history, God has called on His people to wait. In this book, we will examine the lives of a few of these God followers—eight biblical ladies-in-waiting, if you will. These were women who yearned for babies. Women who ached for healing. Women who waited for guidance. Women like you and me.

As we study these women and read their stories in Scripture, we will discover how to handle seasons of delay. If we can't have what we want when we want it, what are we to do while we're waiting? As Christians, we know God's promise of a happy ending through Christ. But what are we supposed to do in between heartache and heaven? Tap our toes? Watch the clock? Pace the carpet of hope until it's worn thin?

The examples of these ladies-in-waiting will instruct us that there is a better way to wait. A way to wait well.

Their lives will teach us about trust and surrender when life feels suspended. They will demonstrate how to handle the daily-ness of waiting and show us actions we can take even when it seems there is nothing we can do. We will find that a pause in our plotline doesn't mean the end of our story, and we'll learn that all waiting has a purpose.

Throughout the book, I share some of my own waiting stories. I'm sure you have your own accounts of delay and disappointment too. Although our stories may differ, we will see that God is present in every tale. He gives us His Word to encourage us when it feels like He's nowhere to be found. He promises His nearness when it seems our prayers are not heard. And by the power of God the Holy Spirit through our Baptism, we have faith to trust in His timing and provision.

Although we may detest waiting and struggle greatly with it, ultimately we find that it has the power to draw us to Jesus. One of the best places to meet God is *in the in-between.*

Using This Study

In *Waiting,* you will get to know biblical women who experienced delay. Some of their stories span many chapters of the Bible, some only a few verses. All of them offer fascinating peeks into ancient life. To help you understand each woman's time period, the chapters include the following:

- **timelines** to help you see how each woman's life fits in history
- **maps** to give you geographical perspective of her home
- **historical information** to help you envision the life she may have lived

You may choose to explore the concept of waiting well by reading the book straight through. Or you may take the time to go deeper by engaging in the Bible study questions in the back of the book beginning on page 147. These questions will help you reflect on the reading, dive into Scripture, and apply the lessons to your own life. There are even a few creative projects to help you internalize the concepts.

I encourage you to study *Waiting* with a group. Gather a few waiting women together. Learn from the biblical women of the past—that's why God includes their stories in Scripture. Support one another as you wait in the present—especially when it may feel like God isn't there. As you share with one another your own waiting stories of financial difficulties, relationship struggles, or health problems, you will be encouraged to see how God works in every life.

As you study with your group, remember these guidelines:

- Begin and end your time together with prayer.
- Rely on Scripture to guide your discussions.
- Keep what is shared confidential unless given permission to share outside the group.

May God bless you as you learn to wait well.

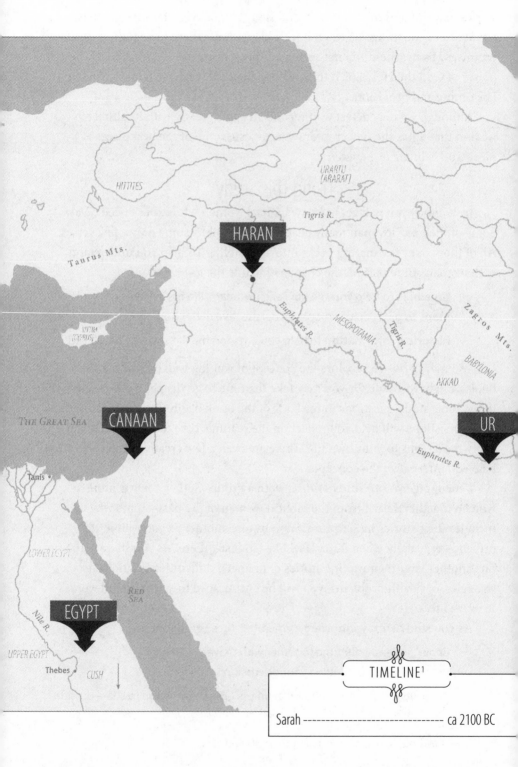

HITTITES

URARTU
[ARARAT]

Tigris R.

HARAN

Taurus Mts.

Euphrates R.

MESOPOTAMIA

Tigris R.

Zagros Mts.

BABYLONIA

AKKAD

KITTIM
[CYPRUS]

THE GREAT SEA

CANAAN

UR

Euphrates R.

Tanis

LOWER EGYPT

RED SEA

EGYPT

Nile R.

UPPER EGYPT

Thebes

CUSH

TIMELINE[1]

Sarah ------------------------------- ca 2100 BC

Chapter 1

Sarah

I have done a lot of do-it-yourself projects in my day.

As a teenager, I used my sewing machine to reproduce the cute outfits I saw in my favorite store but couldn't afford. While in college, I taught myself to cook. (Well, that might be a bit of an overstatement.) As a newlywed, I tried to feather our nest with furniture I refinished myself—even snatching pieces with potential from the curbs on garbage day.

My husband and I took on a huge do-it-yourself project when we built our own home. We relied on the experts to pour the foundation, frame the house, and install plumbing and electricity, but my husband installed insulation, laid shingles, and constructed interior carpentry. I painted dozens of walls and varnished miles of woodwork.

But there was one thing we couldn't seem to complete on our own: children. What should have been the easiest thing for a loving husband and wife to attain continued to stay just out of reach for us. As all of our friends welcomed their bundles of joy, our arms remained empty. And we wondered, *Why is God making us wait?*

I'm sure that Sarah, wife of the Old Testament patriarch Abraham, also asked herself that question. After all, God had promised Abraham a son. Why was He making them wait? Eventually, Sarah grew tired of the delay and tried a do-it-yourself plan that resulted in disaster. Instead of waiting for God's timing in her life, she took matters into her own hands—and ended up wishing she hadn't.

Setting the Scene

Sarah was born ca. 2156 BC, and when we first meet her, she is living in the Sumerian city of Ur. Her name at the beginning of the story is Sarai, which means "my princess." Since Ur was a thriving metropolitan area and her father appeared to be fairly wealthy, I can imagine Sarai was treated like royalty.

We know Sarai was very beautiful because even when she was a senior citizen, her husband, Abram, worried that important kings would want her for their harems (Genesis 12:11–13; 20:1–2). He was so afraid a willful ruler would kill him to attain her that he told the kings Sarai was his sister.

We don't know much about Abram and Sarai's early life. Perhaps they were educated, flourishing citizens of the great city of Ur. Perhaps they attended grand parties and important festivals.

THE ANCIENT CITY OF UR

There is some debate about the exact location of Ur, but many scholars place it on the River Euphrates near the Persian Gulf. Because of the silting of the Euphrates, the site is now 150 miles inland, but during Abraham's time it was an important port city. In fact, it may have been the greatest city-state in the world at that time. It was a prosperous industrial, agricultural, and commercial center with a population of 200,000–300,000. The city was dominated by a great brick ziggurat that honored the moon god Nanna. Middle-class families lived in houses with ten to twenty rooms. They enjoyed the availability of plenty of food and good education.[2]

We do know Abram and Sarai's father, Terah, worshiped other gods (Joshua 24:2). Maybe he, like other citizens of Ur, bowed down to Nanna, the popular moon god. But Abram was called by Yahweh—the one true God:

> Now the Lord said to Abram, "Go from your country and your kindred and your father's house to the land that I will show you."
> Genesis 12:1

I wonder, how did Abram come to know Yahweh in a land of idols? How did he hear the voice of the Lord in a place filled with cries to moon gods? We aren't told the details of the call of Abram. Neither are we told how Abram shared God's words with Sarai. I, for one, would have liked to have eavesdropped on *that* conversation. Did Abram come in the back door and greet Sarai as she was making bread?

Were Sarai's hands suddenly still when Abram relayed God's instructions to leave Ur? Did she stop kneading the dough, put her hands on her hips and question, "And where did God say we should move?"

Did her jaw drop when Abram replied, "He hasn't shared that little detail with me yet"?

God told Abram to leave his country (Genesis 12:1) and flee all influences that led to false gods. Scripture tells us:

> Terah took Abram his son and Lot the son of Haran, his grandson, and Sarai his daughter-in-law, his son Abram's wife, and they went forth together from Ur of the Chaldeans to go into the land of Canaan, but when they came to Haran, they settled there.
>
> Genesis 11:31

BROTHER AND SISTER?

Abram wasn't lying when he told the rulers that Sarai was his sister. She actually was his half sister—both were children of Terah. At this time in history, marriage between brother and sister was not forbidden. God gave the law prohibiting relations between siblings in Leviticus 20:17—about seven hundred years after Abram. If you think about it, at the beginning of the world, such marriage was necessary. The daughters and sons of Adam and Eve had no other marriage prospects.[3]

Abram and all of his household set out on the long journey. But after

A PUZZLE

Genesis 11:31 tells us Terah, Abram, Sarai, and company set off for the land of Canaan, but in Genesis 12:1, God does not give a specific destination. Acts 7:2–3 confirms that God first called Abram in Ur: "The God of glory appeared to our father Abraham when he was in Mesopotamia, before he lived in Haran, and said to him, 'Go out from your land and from your kindred and go into the land that I will show you.'" How do we reconcile the two passages?

One commentary suggests that when Genesis 11:31 tells us they set off for the land of Canaan, this was "expressive of the Divine destination, rather than of the conscious intention of the travelers".[4] The Bible summarizes what is going to happen.

approximately six hundred miles of arduous travel, they stopped in Haran. We are not sure why they cut the journey short, but commentators suggest that it may have been because of Terah's health.

But Haran was not their final destination. Haran was in between what Abram and Sarai had left behind and where God wanted them to go. It was a waiting place. However, God did not give up on them. He continues to call His people when they are not totally obedient. So when Terah died at the age of 205, Abram and Sarai

THE COST OF OBEDIENCE

Abram and Sarai left a stable, prosperous life in Ur for a nomadic, unsettled life in Canaan. Out of obedience to God, they traded in a comfortable home in a thriving city for a series of tents in a foreign land. Instead of being part of a society filled with family and friends, they were strangers and outsiders in an unfamiliar location.[5]

packed their bags again and completed the journey God had instructed them to take, traveling three hundred more miles to Canaan. By this time, Sarai was a senior citizen (she was 65, and Abram was 75). If I had been Sarai, I would have complained about another move so late in life. I would have grumbled about living in tents and about sand in my soup. But we have no indication that Sarai did that. In fact, in the New Testament, the apostle Peter commended Sarah as an obedient wife (1 Peter 3:5–6).

Waiting for a Child

All this time, Sarai was not only waiting for a place to settle down; she was also waiting for a child. The very first description of her is "Now Sarai was barren; she had no child" (Genesis 11:30). How would you like to be introduced as "Sarai, mother of none"? Parents of young children are often known as "Ethan's mom" or "Emma's dad," but Sarai was defined by her lack of children. That had to hurt.

And it was probably very confusing because when God told Abram he should pick up and move, He also promised, "I will make of you a great nation" (Genesis 12:2). Now, a great nation doesn't appear out of thin air. So years earlier when Abram shared this promise with Sarai, she probably envisioned being the mother of a great brood of offspring.

But she waited and waited. She waited through a move away from the homeland she knew. Waited through a journey to Haran. Waited through the trip to Canaan. Even waited through a tour of Egypt. And everywhere they went, God blessed them with material wealth. Abram became "very rich in livestock, in silver, and in gold" (Genesis 13:2), but Sarai still didn't have the one thing her heart ached for—a child.

After living in Canaan for some years, God visited Abram in a vision and gave him a more specific promise: "Your very own son shall be your heir" (Genesis 15:4). God called Abram out to look at the night sky and promised that his descendants would be as countless as the stars in the heavens.

Abram and Sarai had probably given up on the possibility of having children. Perhaps they had often lamented the fact that there were no little ones to play peekaboo with the tent flaps. No babies to hold. No toddlers to hug. But now, God resurrected hope in their hearts.

POLYGAMY IN THE BIBLE

God's plan for marriage has always been one man, one woman: "Therefore a man shall leave his father and his mother and hold fast to his wife, and they shall become one flesh" (Genesis 2:24). But during ancient times, polygamy was widely practiced. Lamech was the first man to marry two wives (Genesis 4:19). He was not a man of good character. He killed a man for striking him (Genesis 4:23). Abram was the first godly man reported to have multiple wives.

A Do-It-Yourself Project

However, this is where things started to go wrong. After Sarai and Abram had been living in Canaan for ten years, Sarai decided she had waited long enough. At this point, she was seventy-five years old, and surely her body had given her all the signs that babies were no longer a possibility. She remembered God's promise that Abram would have a son, but perhaps she despaired that God made no direct mention of her. She told her husband, "The Lord has prevented me from bearing children. Go in to my servant; it may be that I shall obtain children by her" (Genesis 16:2). It was like she was saying, "Abram, it looks like we have to go with Plan B. If God isn't going to give me children, it seems a surrogate is my only path to motherhood. So go sleep with my maid."

Right. Accomplish God's plan by violating the sacred gift of marriage.

Sarai was definitely not waiting well.

Sarai must have been extremely desperate by this time to suggest sharing her husband with another woman. But maybe she had already asked all of her neighbors for their homemade remedies. Perhaps she had visited the local herbalist and picked up every fertility potion available.

Sarai tried waiting for God. She had waited for years since the Lord had first vowed Abram would have countless descendants. Maybe she thought, *Why hasn't God blessed us with a child when He so clearly promised one? It's probably all my fault. I don't know what I've done to deserve God's anger. But there's no reason Abram should suffer for my mistakes. We can't wait forever. If God isn't going to bless me with a child of my own, my little do-it-yourself project with Hagar should work instead.*

Surprisingly (or maybe not so surprisingly), Abram agreed to Sarai's plan. And it worked. Hagar became pregnant. But it wasn't long before Sarai regretted her decision. Once Hagar knew she was pregnant, she openly despised Sarai. She knew she could do something her mistress couldn't.

Thirteen more years go by. Sarai has now had more than a decade of living with the consequences of her choice. Can you imagine Sarai sitting in the shade of the entrance to her tent and watching as Abram walked with Ishmael? Did she feel a stab of pain in her heart when Abram put his arm around his son—by another woman? Did she glance over to the cooking fire and see Hagar also observing the scene with a smile on her face? Sarai's name was "My Princess." She may have been accustomed to getting everything she wanted. But the one thing she most desired, she couldn't have. And now, at the age of eighty-nine . . .

Sarai had probably resigned herself to the fact that God had promised Abram a son.

But not her.

Then the Lord came to Abram again. Thirteen years after Ishmael was born, God once again told Abram that he would be the father of many, even changing his name from *Abram* ("exalted father") to *Abraham* ("father of many"). And this time, the Lord specifically mentioned Sarai. He changed her name—from *Sarai* to *Sarah*. Both mean "princess," perhaps emphasizing that she would become the mother of rulers and kings.[6] The Lord assured Abraham a son would be born within a year, and Sarah would share in the blessing:

> "As for Sarai your wife, you shall not call her name Sarai, but Sarah shall be her name. I will bless her, and moreover, I will give you a son by her. I will bless her, and she shall become nations; kings of peoples shall come from her."
>
> Genesis 17:15–16

At this, Abraham fell facedown and laughed. Was he responding with temporary disbelief? Was the laughter a response of incredulous joy at the thought of having a child at the age of one hundred? Or was he responding to the irony that now that he and Sarah had lived through the consequences of her flawed DIY project, God was revealing the fact that Sarah had been part of the plan all along?

Shortly after God's visit with Abraham, Sarah met the Lord herself. She had waited a long time to be included in the promise. At last, Sarah encountered this mysterious God who, for decades, had dangled the promise of a child in front of her but never allowed her to catch it.

The visit took place at their home. While Abraham sat at the entrance of his tent, he looked up and saw three men. Recognizing one of them as the Lord, he immediately urged them to stay awhile. He instructed Sarah to bake some bread while he selected a calf for the meal and directed a servant to prepare the meat. While the Lord ate, Abraham stood near them and Sarah eavesdropped on the conversation, hiding at the entrance of the tent. When God repeated His promise that Sarah would have a son within a year, Sarah laughed to herself and thought, *Are you kidding? Now that I'm old and worn out? Now I'm going to be a mother?*

The promise had become more specific. Now God revealed His timeline: a son would be born within a year. Wouldn't you like it if God told you exactly when He was going to answer your prayer? But I think Sarah had waited so long and had hoped so long, that now she simply couldn't let herself believe the good news. She had heard it before and nothing had happened. Perhaps she didn't want to get her hopes up again only to be disappointed once more.

God heard Sarah laugh, and she tried to deny her silent snickers—after all, she had "laughed to herself" (Genesis 18:12). She had expressed her doubts only in her thoughts. It must have been a bit disconcerting when the Lord said, "No, but you did laugh" (Genesis 18:15). How could He know what was in her head and in her heart?

Is Anything Too Hard for the Lord?

It was then that God asked the question at the heart of the matter: "Is anything too hard for the LORD?" (Genesis 18:14).

Behind that question are a dozen others: Don't you believe I am powerful enough to give you a child? Don't you trust Me to provide what you need? Don't you see it all depends on Me and not on you?

Ah, there is the crux. It certainly looks like Sarah believed everything hinged on her efforts. We see this in her very first words recorded in Scripture:

> And Sarai said to Abram, "Behold now, the LORD has prevented me from bearing children. Go in to my servant; it may be that I shall obtain children by her."
>
> Genesis 16:2

In the Hebrew narrative, the first words a person speaks reveal his or her character and personality. Sarah's first recorded words happen here in Genesis 16 and in them we see Sarah's impatience. When God didn't meet her expectations, Sarah decided not to wait for God's timing. She blamed God for her misfortune—"the LORD has prevented me from bearing children"—and didn't trust Him to come through on the promise to Abram.

Now believe me, I can relate. I have already told you how I like do-it-yourself projects. Maybe you do too. There is a certain satisfaction in creating something with your own two hands. A particular pride that comes when you've accomplished something with your own efforts.

And that's the problem. See that little word in the last sentence—*pride*? From the beginning of time, we humans have tried to convince ourselves we don't need God. We can manage by ourselves, thank you very much. Satan told Adam and Eve they didn't have to depend on God for knowledge— they could become wise *like* Him. The ancient world tried to prove their independence and ingenuity by building a tower to the heavens (Genesis 11).

But God designed us to need Him. He has constructed the universe in a way that reveals His limitless power and rule and our limited understanding and ability. In the account of Abraham and Sarah, God continually reminded them that He is the Almighty. He is the one in control.

The very first encounter between the citizen of Ur and the Lord demonstrated this. God told Abram, "Leave all that is familiar and follow Me. Trust Me for the next step and the next step and the next, and don't be concerned about your final destination. Depend on Me and not on your maps or guides." Yahweh wanted Abram—and Sarai—to abandon control of their own existence and let Him choose the path of their lives.

Yahweh wanted Abram—and Sarai—to abandon control of their own existence and let Him choose the path of their lives.

The Lord reminded Abram of His might once again when He reiterated His promise in Genesis 17:

> When Abram was ninety-nine years old the LORD appeared to Abram and said to him, "I am God Almighty; walk before Me, and be blameless, that I may make My covenant between Me and you, and may multiply you greatly."
>
> Genesis 17:1-2

Here God revealed Himself with a new name—God Almighty. The Hebrew is *El-Shaddai*, which "perhaps means 'God, the Mountain One,' either highlighting the invincible power of God or referring to the mountains as God's symbolic home."[7] God, the One-with-All-the-Might, would fulfill the promise.

Again, God reminded Abram and Sarai that He was the one with the power. He was the one in control.

But somehow that lesson never sank in with Sarah. She executed a do-it-yourself plan that backfired. She laughed when God reassured her she would have a child in a year's time.

What God Is Waiting For

I can so relate to Sarah taking the initiative. I'm all about planning and accomplishing important tasks. But I can also connect with her desperate yearning for children and the frustration of waiting for that bundle of joy.

That prolonged period of waiting came when I was a newlywed. My husband and I were married as students. Actually, we took turns being students. John worked at a local church while I finished my bachelor's degree; then I worked as a seamstress and piano teacher while he finished seminary. And all the while we were *waiting* for the time when we would be finished with school and get on with the business of our careers and starting a family.

Finally, the last year of seminary came. We could hardly wait for the year to be over. We barely contained the anticipation we felt while wondering where John's first congregation would be. Would it be someplace exciting, like New York? Or would we be able to stay close to family in the Midwest?

We were totally unprepared when John got the news that his first church would be in Missoula, Montana. I mean—Montana! Having never been there, my first thought was, *If it's not the end of the earth, you can certainly see it from there!* Somehow I pictured us as pioneer pastor and wife crossing the prairie in a covered wagon, settling in a remote town without any ties to modern civilization.

But later, when I remembered how much we had prayed about where John would be called, I knew that God would work through us—even in Montana.

So we packed up our belongings and drove three days to get to Missoula—which turned out to be a gorgeous place in the Rocky Mountains. We rented a cute little house on the side of one of those mountains that had a million-dollar view of the city and surrounding peaks. For better or for worse, we were in Montana, ready to start our new lives. At least the waiting was over.

Or so we thought.

Actually, the worst waiting period of our lives was just beginning.

Now that we were finished with schooling, we decided it was time to start a family. And, of course, we assumed that once we decided to do this, it would automatically happen. It would be exactly like signing up for a class—make the commitment and you're in.

But that is *not* what happened. Instead we had more waiting. *Months* went by—and nothing happened. Can you tell I'm an impatient person?

Finally, one month, I suspected God had answered our prayers, but I also began to have some unusual pain. A trip to the doctor confirmed that yes, I was pregnant, but there was also a chance I would lose the baby.

A couple of weeks later, that's exactly what happened. Any of you who have had a miscarriage know what a heartache it is.

People told us, "Don't worry, you're young. You'll get pregnant again." But this time the wait was even longer. And all the while, we seemed to get a baby shower invitation or a birth announcement in the mail every week.

All of our friends were having babies—but our nursery was still empty.

There were doctor visits and tests and thermometers and tests and carefully timed romance and . . . more tests. But in the end, I had to come to the point where I acknowledged, "Lord, it's all up to You. You are the one who's in control."

Many times in my life, God has brought me to this point. The point where I have tried and failed. Tried and failed again. Usually, like some badly stained laundry, it takes many cycles of trying and failing before I finally throw up my hands and say, "Okay, Lord. It's not working. I can't do it. I guess I'm just going to have to trust You. Thy will be done."

Hmm. Can't you hear God saying, "That's what *I've* been waiting for"?

Maybe that's what was going on with Sarah's long wait. Perhaps God waited and waited and waited to bless Sarah with a child until it was obvious to everyone that the child was all His doing. God did not bless Abraham and Sarah with a child because they followed all the directions. It wasn't because their plan showed ingenuity. It wasn't because they demonstrated they would be perfect parents or even because they were perfectly faithful to Him. They received the blessing of a child only because of God's miraculous power and grace and because His will for a Savior would be fulfilled through the child.

Finally, Sarah, at the age of ninety, gave birth to a son and named him Isaac. *Isaac* means "laughter." Kind of ironic, don't you think? Actually, the name Isaac was God's idea (Genesis 17:19). Although Sarah expressed skeptical giggles before, God used the name Laughter to celebrate the joy

SARAH'S TIMELINE	
ca. 2156 BC	Sarai born
ca. ?	Leaves Ur
ca. 2091 BC	Moves to Canaan
ca. 2081 BC	DIY project
ca. 2080 BC	Ishmael born
ca. 2067 BC	God visits Sarah
ca. 2066 BC	Isaac is born
ca. 2029 BC	Sarah dies

of a long-awaited son of promise. Sarah herself now had a different kind of laughter: "And Sarah said, 'God has made laughter for me; everyone who hears will laugh over me.' And she said, 'Who would have said to Abraham that Sarah would nurse children? Yet I have borne him a son in his old age'" (Genesis 21:6–7).

You know what? These words are Sarah's only optimistic words recorded. All of the other times she speaks in Genesis, it is negative. First, she tells Abram to sleep with her maid (Genesis 16:2). Then, she *blames* Abram for sleeping with her maid (Genesis 16:5). (Anyone see that coming?) She scoffs at God's words (Genesis 18:12). Finally, she lies to God about her laughter (Genesis 18:15).

Clearly, Sarah is not someone to emulate when we are faced with a long wait. And yet our Lord demonstrates His grace in the life of Sarah. She was not selected to be the mother of Isaac and the nation of Israel because she was perfect. She wasn't picked because she would be the strongest, most energetic mother. (Can you imagine chasing after a toddler at ninety-two?) God chose her out of His grace—for her and for us.

The What and How and Why of Waiting

Sarah is famous for her long wait. And infamous for her rash actions when she grew tired of waiting. She abandoned her trust in God and put her confidence in her own ingenuity.

Been there. Done that. I could have a hundred T-shirts commemorating my tendency to step ahead of God and try to fix things on my own. I've attempted to repair a relationship with my own comments instead of turning to God for the right words to say. I've said yes to a new volunteer opportunity before first asking the Father if those plans fit into His.

And regrettably, I often follow my own DIY project until it falls apart in my hands. Usually, I don't tap into God's grace until my self-sufficiency has proven useless.

You too? We probably all relate to Sarah. Our long waiting periods often drive us to try something—anything—that will heal our pain or fix our problems. Discouragement multiplies. Frustration escalates. Anger intensifies. We fall into First Commandment sins: doubting our loving God and questioning His timing. Trust runs dry and we think, *If God won't, then I will.*

But we can learn from Sarah too. We can learn that nothing is too hard for the Lord. We can realize He specializes in coming through when everything appears hopeless to us.

When I read Sarah's story, I wonder if God included it to demonstrate that when life seems to be nothing but a dreadfully long wait, we need to change our perspective. Instead of viewing a pause in our plans as an inconvenience or as a disappointment or as an excuse to step out of God's will, He wants us to interpret it as an opportunity to grow in trust. A time to relax and watch the Almighty work. A chance to grab on to the Lord's rhetorical question "Is anything too hard for the Lord?" and respond with a resounding "No!"

Isaiah 26:8 says:

> In the path of Your judgments, O Lord, we wait for You; Your name and remembrance are the desire of our soul.

This verse is a miniature textbook on waiting well. It teaches us the what and how and why of waiting.

What are we to do while waiting? We are to follow "the path of [God's] judgments." We are to observe God's laws. Obey His Word. Trust in His provision. Don't try any DIY projects that are contradictory to Scripture. Do what God has already instructed us to do—and no more.

How do we wait? The New American Standard Bible translates Isaiah 26:8 as "We have waited for You eagerly." I don't know about you, but I am not *eager* to wait. I'm not wild about waiting for a loved one to return to the fellowship of a Christian church. I don't choose extended periods of uncertainty when I'm searching for purpose. I don't jump at the chance to languish in pain if my health suffers. But when I looked up the Hebrew for this verse, I was relieved that the word *eagerly* doesn't mean to be excited about waiting. Instead it means "to look eagerly for." We are not to wait with feelings of hopelessness or impatience. We aren't meant to dwell in a pessimistic attitude, thinking, *God will never come through for me.* Waiting well means enthusiastically anticipating what God is going to do—even if He chooses a different plan from our own. It means praying, "Thy will be done."

Why do we wait? We wait because what we want more than anything is for God's name to be glorified. His "name and remembrance are the desire of our soul" (Isaiah 26:8). When we attempt do-it-yourself projects, we are flaunting what we can do. But when we wait for God to act, we are giving God a chance to show us what He can do. Waiting until the age of ninety to have a child wasn't easy for Sarah. But certainly God received all the credit. God allows "in-between times" to give us opportunities to trust. To demonstrate there is nothing too hard for Him. He wants nothing more than for us to let go of our projects, our schemes, and our self-sufficiency and allow Him to work.

When I read Sarah's story, I imagine her remorse over her do-it-yourself project made her wonder what life would have been like if she had simply waited for God's timing. She must have been miserable in her doubt. She probably wished she had picked up on all of the Lord's reminders that He was

> Instead of viewing a pause in our plans as an inconvenience or as a disappointment or as an excuse to step out of God's will, He wants us to interpret it as an opportunity to grow in trust.

> God wants nothing more than for us to let go of our projects, our schemes, and our self-sufficiency and allow Him to work.

the one in control. Most likely, she regretted laughing at God's promise.

I admit, I've been like Sarah in my doubt and impatience. How many times have I ignored God's amazing plans and tried to force my own agenda? How many times have I elbowed my way past His design for my life, only to experience disappointment and frustration?

What DIY project have you been attempting in your life? Demanding your way in your marriage? (Ahem. I resemble that remark.) Ignoring God's leading and insisting on your own life plan? (Yep, I've done that too.) Relying on your own energy as you pursue your career? (Sorry, Lord.) God is asking us to let it all go.

Nothing is too hard for the Lord. He longs to demonstrate that in our lives.

God's Grace in Sarah's Story

Sarah could have been labeled simply as "An Example of What Not to Do While Waiting." But God identifies her as an example of faith.

In Genesis, Sarah is portrayed as both doubting and pouting. But in Hebrews 11:11, we read, "By faith Sarah herself received power to conceive, even when she was past the age, since she considered Him faithful who had promised."

It seems that after the DIY project, the Lord worked faith in her heart. And here in the New Testament, it appears God has totally forgotten about her complaining, her doubting, and her conniving. She is commended for her trust. There is no reference to her laughing at God's promise. No footnote reminding us of her failed plan. Instead, we are reminded of God's power and fulfilled promises—to Sarah in the birth of Isaac, and to us in the birth of our Savior.

What reassurance of God's grace! I don't have to be remembered for my own failed DIY projects. Because of the saving work of Jesus, God invites me to repent of my efforts to craft a life of my own making and receive His forgiveness. Through the work of the Holy Spirit, He erases my self-sufficiency and imparts faith in His amazing power. In Christ, the Father sees me only as His forgiven and redeemed child.

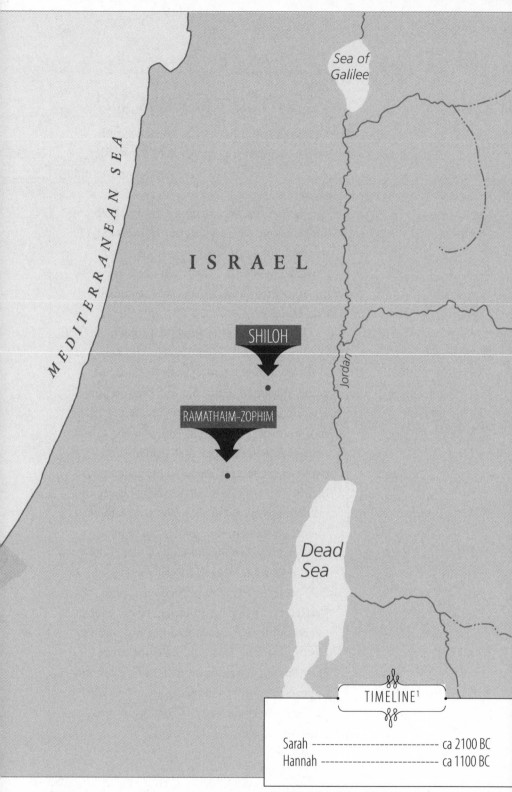

Sea of
Galilee

MEDITERRANEAN SEA

ISRAEL

SHILOH

RAMATHAIM-ZOPHIM

Jordan

Dead
Sea

TIMELINE[1]

Sarah ----------------------------- ca 2100 BC
Hannah ----------------------------- ca 1100 BC

Map © iStock / Peter Hermes Furian

Hannah

Chapter 2

When Waiting Means Letting Go

1 Samuel 1–2

It seems much of my life is spent waiting in lines.

I wait in line to check out at the grocery store. I stand in a queue to be served at the bank. And I cringe when it's time to renew my driver's license. Not only do I have to pose for yet another (ahem) not-so-flattering photo, but I have to wait in line to do it.

And whatever line I'm in, it always seems the other lines are moving faster. People who arrived after me are on their way to their cars before I have even placed my groceries on the conveyor belt or reached the teller's window.

The Old Testament woman Hannah may have also despaired as she waited in the much more significant line marked "For Children." She was doing everything right: obeying Jewish law, marrying a respectable man, and waiting for the blessing of a baby. But doing everything right wasn't getting her what she desperately wanted.

It was as if she dutifully pulled the slip of paper from the machine marked "Take a number, please" and patiently waited her turn, but everyone else's number was called first. In fact, her rival, Peninnah, had several turns at motherhood before Hannah even had one chance.

Hannah had the same problem that Sarah suffered. Both women desperately wanted babies of their own. Each watched her husband have children with another woman. But instead of trying to control the situation as Sarah did, Hannah responded with deep confidence in God's goodness. Her trust in the Lord was so profound that she surrendered her desire for children.

I have a soft spot in my heart for Hannah because I also waited in a long line for children. And like this Old Testament woman, I was prompted to

Hannah **25**

release one of my children into His care. God asked me to sacrifice a desire that I felt was vital to my happiness.

Setting the Scene

Hannah lived in the land of Israel during the time of the judges, after the children of Israel had entered the Promised Land. Moses and Joshua were both gone, and the nation was periodically led by judges God appointed when things in the country were getting desperate. It was a dark

The Times of the Judges	
1399–1375 BC	Death of Joshua and the elders
1209–1169 BC	Deborah
1162–1122 BC	Gideon
1157 BC	Eli born
1105 BC	Samuel born
1075–1055 BC	Samson

period in Israel's history, when everyone not only "did what was right in his own eyes" (Judges 17:6) but also "did what was evil in the sight of the LORD" (2:11). Anarchy ran rampant. Religious, political, and moral values vanished.[2]

It is in this darkness that Hannah stands out like a ray of light. Her piety and devotion are in stark contrast to the godlessness of the age.

Hannah was born around 1080 BC. Her story begins in 1 Samuel 1:

> There was a certain man of Ramathaim-zophim of the hill country of Ephraim whose name was Elkanah the son of Jeroham, son of Elihu, son of Tohu, son of Zuph, an Ephrathite. He had two wives. The name of the one was Hannah, and the name of the other, Peninnah. And Peninnah had children, but Hannah had no children.
>
> 1 Samuel 1:1–2

Hannah was married to a man named Elkanah. We know from a genealogy in 1 Chronicles 6:16–28 that Elkanah was from the tribe of Levi and, more specifically, of the Kohathite clan. Later, David would put this important clan in charge of worship music in the temple. Elkanah's distinction as an Ephrathite here in 1 Samuel refers to his place of residence and not his tribal ancestry. Levites were not given large tracts of property in the Promised Land like other tribes because their inheritance was the Lord Himself. Instead, descendants of Levi were given towns inside the territories of other tribes. Elkanah and Hannah lived in Ramathaim-zophim in the hill country of Ephraim—a town approximately twenty-two miles north of Jerusalem.[3]

Right away we find out Hannah was not Elkanah's only wife. Most likely Hannah was his first wife, but when she couldn't have children, he might have married another woman to carry on the family line. And we know from Sarah's story that this practice leads to nothing but trouble.

The drama opens with a family trip to Shiloh for the yearly sacrifice. Scripture tells us Elkanah "used to go up year by year from his city to worship and to sacrifice to the LORD of hosts at Shiloh" (1

SHILOH

Shiloh was a famous city of Ephraim, north of Jerusalem and south of Shechem. After the people of Israel entered Canaan, the tabernacle was set up there. The ark and the tabernacle continued at Shiloh, from 1444 BC to 1116 BC, when it was taken by the Philistines, under the administration of the high priest Eli.[4]

Samuel 1:3). Commentators suggest that the occasion here was the Feast of Tabernacles, or Booths, when the people of Israel all came to the tabernacle and camped out in booths or tents to remember their time of wandering in the wilderness. Part of this festival was a required sacrifice. Each family brought their own animal to sacrifice. Portions of the animal were burned on the altar to God and other parts were reserved for the priests. But some of the meat was given back to the family to be eaten in an area near the tabernacle. It was a joyous time of feasting and fellowship

But it wasn't joyful for Hannah. Peninnah, Elkanah's other wife, "used to provoke her grievously to irritate her, because the LORD had closed her womb" (1 Samuel 1:6). Wife Number Two took every opportunity possible to get under Wife Number One's skin. You can almost see the scene playing out. Elkanah came back from the altar and gave Peninnah and each of her sons and daughters a portion of the meat. Peninnah probably bustled around her offspring, making sure to emphasize the fact that she had children and Hannah didn't.

I can see Hannah's eyes fill with tears. She tries to brush them away before anyone notices. She scolds herself under her breath, "You were going to stay strong this year. You weren't going to let that woman get to you this time."

Most likely Elkanah saw all that was going on, but he wasn't sure what he could do. He gave Hannah a double portion of meat, but Hannah didn't touch it. There was a lump in her throat preventing any food, no matter how special, from going down. Elkanah tried to comfort her by saying, "Hannah, why do you weep? And why do you not eat? And why is your heart sad? Am I not more to you than ten sons?" (1 Samuel 1:8).

Finally, Hannah could take no more. She got up and walked toward the tabernacle court. Passing the blue, purple, and scarlet screen, she entered the court and knelt to talk to the Lord. She knew He was the one who understood her heart. He was the one who could satisfy her deep desires.

Once away from Peninnah, Hannah let the tears flow. She poured out her heart to God:

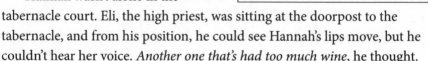

"O LORD of hosts, if You will indeed look on the affliction of Your servant and remember me and not forget Your servant, but will give to Your servant a son, then I will give him to the LORD all the days of his life, and no razor shall touch his head." 1 Samuel 1:11

THE TABERNACLE

The Hebrew word for "tabernacle," *mishkan*, means "dwelling place." When the people of Israel were on their journey to Canaan, God instructed Moses to create a tabernacle that would be His dwelling place during their years of wandering. It had an exterior court measuring 150 x 75 feet, constructed with curtains of twined linen (Exodus 27:9). Upon entering the court, the worshiper would first encounter a huge bronze altar 7.5 feet long and wide and 4.5 feet high. After the altar was the tabernacle itself. It was 30 feet long and 15 feet wide and was made of curtains of finely twisted linen with blue, purple, and scarlet yarn. Any Israelite could enter the tabernacle court, but only the priests could enter the tabernacle itself.[5]

Hannah wasn't alone in the tabernacle court. Eli, the high priest, was sitting at the doorpost to the tabernacle, and from his position, he could see Hannah's lips move, but he couldn't hear her voice. *Another one that's had too much wine*, he thought. But when he confronted her, Hannah assured him she hadn't had any strong drink. She told the priest, "I have been pouring out my soul before the LORD. Do not regard your servant as a worthless woman, for all along I have been speaking out of my great anxiety and vexation" (1 Samuel 1:15–16).

Eli's mistake might be explained by the general decline in Israel's morals. In fact, during this period of time, his own sons were known to have sexual relations with the women who served at the temple (1 Samuel 2:22). Perhaps Eli thought Hannah was one of those women.

But to Eli's credit, once he realized his mistake, he gave Hannah a blessing: "Go in peace, and the God of Israel grant your petition that you have made to Him" (1 Samuel 1:17). This was not a prophecy, but it was a word of God to be received in faith.[6]

Now that Hannah had poured out her heart to God, "her face was no longer sad," and she told Eli, "Let your servant find favor in your eyes" (1 Samuel 1:18); then she rose and returned to her family. Now she was finally able to eat some of the festival meal. A woman of great faith, Hannah laid all of her troubles at the Lord's feet and trusted Him to act.

The next morning the whole family rose early to worship one more time before they went back to Ramah. And "in due time" Hannah did become pregnant and give birth to a son. She named him Samuel, which in Hebrew sounds like "heard of God" (1 Samuel 1:20). The Lord had listened to Hannah's cries and answered them.

Not long after the birth of Samuel, it was time to go back to the temple for the yearly sacrifice. Hannah begged off. She told her husband, "As soon as the child is weaned, I will bring him, so that he may appear in the presence of the LORD and dwell there forever" (1 Samuel 1:22). Elkanah agreed.

Three years later (most Israelite children were weaned at age 3), Hannah made the trip back to Shiloh to fulfill her vow to the Lord. Amazing. After waiting years for a child, she kept her promise and gave Samuel back to God. Scripture tells us she visited Samuel every year and brought him a special handmade robe. But she no longer saw her young son every day. She willingly surrendered her heart's desire for children to the almighty God.

Can you imagine? For three years, she fed Samuel. She soothed him when he was hurt and comforted him when he was sad. She cradled him in her arms and taught him about Yahweh, who answered her prayers. She nursed him and recounted the stories of Noah and Abraham and Moses. Now she would no longer tuck him into bed at night or hear him call out "Mother" in

NAZIRITE VOW

When Hannah adds the phrase "no razor shall touch his head" to her vow, she is referencing the Nazirite vow described in Numbers 6. This was a special vow made to dedicate oneself to the Lord for a specific period of time. There were three requirements for this vow:

- Abstaining from wine and all products of the grapevine

- Letting the hair grow ("no razor shall touch his head")

- Avoiding contact with the dead

Usually this vow of dedication was for a limited length of time, but Hannah dedicates her future son to God for his whole life.

INCLUSIO

Hannah's story uses a literary device called an *inclusio*—a section of text formed using the same word or phrase both at the beginning and the end. This word highlights the meaning of the section. It gives us clues on how to interpret the text.[7] In Hannah's story, the word *sacrifice* appears both in 1 Samuel 1:3 and in 2:19, where the narrator describes how Hannah's family journeys to Shiloh to worship and sacrifice to the Lord.

the morning. Hannah left Samuel in the care of Eli. She entrusted him to the protection of the Lord.

I wonder . . . did she kneel down and kiss Samuel when it was time to say good-bye? Did she remind him to be a good boy for Eli? Did she put on a brave face for Samuel and fall apart on the journey home? Scripture doesn't give us these details, but certainly, it would not have been easy to release her source of great joy into the Lord's hands, even if she had promised from the outset that that's exactly what she would do.

Surrender and Sacrifice

Hannah's waiting story is bracketed by accounts of the communal sacrifices that highlight her very personal sacrifice. While everyone else was bringing their sheep, goats, and bulls to the altar, Hannah brought her own dear child. She promised God that if He would bless her with a son, she would give him back. Wow. I am astounded at the courage and devotion it took to keep that vow.

Hannah's deep piety is evident. Her devotion to God stands out in stark contrast to the general abandonment of God's principles in the age of the judges. Perhaps her devotion was nurtured during her long wait. If God had blessed her with many children sooner, would she have been a perfectly content mother but without a deep longing for God? Would her parenting duties have distracted her from her relationship with the Lord?

Hannah's response to the long delay in her life is so different from Sarah's. Unlike Sarah, Hannah waited well. Sarah tried to orchestrate her life according to her own timeframe, but Hannah recognized God as the controller of the universe. This is evident from the beginning of Hannah's prayer (1 Samuel 1:11). She addressed God as the "Lord of hosts" (or "Lord Almighty" in some translations). In Scripture, the word *hosts* usually refers to heavenly bodies like the sun, moon, and stars. But it can also indicate human armies or armies of angels. This name of God emphasizes the sovereignty of God over the whole universe.

Hannah also described herself as God's servant. She came in humility, not insisting on her own way or her own timetable. Perhaps her long wait filtered out any demanding aspects of her nature and left only meekness.

Surely Hannah could have been tempted to endure her long wait with a load of impatience. After all, the line for children she had stepped into never seemed to move. But Hannah realized that God is not a genie she could command. He is the controller of the universe and is not obliged to do what we want, when we want it.

Because Hannah recognized the Lord of hosts, she understood that everything she had and everything she would receive from Yahweh already belonged to Him. Her husband's name was a constant reminder of this fact. *Elkanah* means "God is owner." It was a fitting name for a Levite who would be dedicated to the service of the Lord. Perhaps that name reminded her that if God did bless her with a child, that child would actually belong to God and be on loan to her.

Like Hannah, we give God glory because all we possess is a gift from Him. He is the true owner. When we recognize God as the Lord of hosts, it is easier to hold our possessions and desires loosely.

Surrender Isn't Easy

Still, surrender of our longings isn't child's play. I marvel at Hannah's ability to release her desire for a baby to the Lord. I'm even more astounded by her ability to keep her promise and leave her three-year-old son at the tabernacle—dedicating him to God's service.

I have a special affinity for Hannah's situation because God also asked me to surrender my desires and trust His sufficiency.

After my struggle to have children, God blessed me with two little ones. Our first child was born while we were still living in Montana, so we nicknamed her our Montana Anna. Our son, Nathaniel, was born after we moved back to the Midwest. He's our Illinois Boy.

All that waiting for babies to hold taught me some important lessons. However, those babies eventually grew up. Now, this wasn't exactly a surprise. But it happened way too fast. And somehow I envisioned my grown children living nearby. I remember a conversation I had with my daughter as I was tucking her into bed when she was about four. I said something like, "Anna, you are getting so big! Pretty soon you'll be all grown up!"

And Anna, very serious at the thought of being an adult, looked at me and said, "Mom are there any houses on our street that are empty?" Awww . . . my daughter wanted to live close to me when she grew up.

So imagine my surprise when she got married and moved—to China!

Let me tell you, I did not take this news well. Especially because not only did Anna and her husband move seven thousand miles away, but they had the audacity to take my grandchildren with them! No more chasing giggling toddlers through the halls, snuggling on the couch with them, reading storybooks, or laughing along with Winnie-the-Pooh videos. Now my husband, John, and I would have to settle for playing peekaboo on Skype and getting pictures of our grandchildren through email. As a result, I was about as upbeat as Eeyore on life support.

To be perfectly honest, I was in a big snit with God. And I let all my friends know it. I made sure all my friends heard about my grandchildren in *China*. I gave a faint smile as I told how much I missed them. When others talked about their nearby children or grandchildren, I immediately reminded them of my sad situation by sighing wistfully, "You are so lucky to have them close."

Fortunately, I have very sympathetic friends. They commiserated with me. They said, "Oh, it would kill me to have my kids so far away." One friend even commented that my husband and I were the poster children for empty nesters. He said everyone we knew could say, "At least we don't have it as bad as John and Sharla." Okay—that made me laugh. But I really didn't want to be the poster child (or would that be the poster parent?) for empty nesters. I wanted my children close.

Months went by and I continued my snit with God. In fact, I started getting downright depressed about the whole situation. A few months after my daughter's big move, I was scheduled to speak to some women's groups in Iowa. The events had been arranged earlier in the year, but now I was questioning my ability to perform my part. Because of my deep unhappiness, I wondered how I could possibly smile and speak to an audience when my heart was so heavy.

As I drove across Illinois from the Chicago area to Dubuque, I poured my heart out to God. All the way to Iowa, I complained, "Other grandmothers have their grandchildren in the same city. Is it too much to ask that mine be in the same country or at least on the same continent?" I know. That doesn't sound like a very spiritual thing for a Christian speaker to do on her way to tell others the Good News about Jesus. But I had three hours alone in the car, and I really needed to talk the issue out with God.

God hadn't given me any answer by the time I arrived at the first speaking event, but I felt a little better for airing out my frustrations. Now if God would just provide the strength to finish the task before me and give the words these women needed to hear.

That night I spoke about being a friend of God. In my talk, I told the story of another time in my life when I felt lonely. During that period, the issue had been a lack of close friendships. I had grown apart from some of my friends. Others had let me down.

One day during that solitary time, I had been reading the Bible and telling God about my need for friends. I remember sensing Him whisper to my heart, "Remember, Sharla, I am your Friend. Aren't I enough for you?"

Years later, as I was telling this story to the wonderful women in Iowa, I again heard God shouting to my heart, "Do you hear what you are saying? Do I have to ask you again? Sharla, aren't I enough for you?"

The shouting was so loud, I almost had to interrupt my speech and yell, "Really, Lord, do You have to do this now? I'm a little busy here. Can You speak to me when this presentation is over?"

I believe God was asking me to release my daughter into His care. He wanted me to be like Hannah and surrender my child to His service. But this was the hardest thing God had asked me to do up to this point. I was happy that God had big plans for my daughter and her husband in China. I was excited that they were living out their aspirations and vocations. But I was absolutely despondent that the fulfillment of their dreams meant the loss of mine. My deepest longing was to have my family close (even if they weren't just down the street), and God was asking me to let them go.

I was waiting for God to give me the desire of my heart.

But God was waiting for me to allow Him to transform my heart.

In Waiting, God Can Transform Our Hearts

God can alter our souls while we're waiting on Him. Trusting Him. Relying on Him. But that day in Iowa, I wasn't waiting on God. I was not yet ready to be changed. I was stubbornly holding on to my own plans.

Hannah was different. Her story demonstrates the effects of waiting well.

While waiting, we can learn humility. Hannah brought her request for a child to Yahweh, but she didn't insist on her own way. She addressed God as the Lord of hosts. She declared herself to be God's servant.

I, on the other hand, had not yet learned humility. My prayers were still of the demanding variety. I came to God with the attitude that I deserved the answer I wanted: "Lord, other grandmothers have their grandchildren in the same city. Is it too much to ask that mine be in the same country?" (Subtext: Don't I *deserve* to have things my way?)

God was using this opportunity to teach me humility. To develop the lowly heart of a servant. To gratefully accept the gifts He provides. To not pout when I don't receive everything I want. To realize God is the Lord of hosts—the Controller of the universe—and I am not.

While waiting, we can begin to surrender our desires. When Hannah left Samuel in Eli's care, she said:

> "For this child I prayed; and the LORD hath given me my *petition* which I *asked* of Him: Therefore also I have *lent* him to the LORD; as long as he liveth he shall be *lent* to the LORD. And he worshipped the LORD there."
>
> 1 Samuel 1:27–28 (KJV, emphasis added)

The italicized words in the passage above all come from the same Hebrew root—*sha'al*—which means "to ask" or "to be given" or "to make over to" (with or without request).[8] Hannah did not retain her possession of Samuel but gave him over to the Lord—gave God ownership. She knew it was the Lord who had given her a child, and now she was giving him back. She did what all mothers must eventually do; she just did it sooner.

I, however, was not doing a very good job of letting go. I remember when we took my daughter and her family to the airport to catch their flight to China. It was a continuous effort to shove back the tears that were so close to the surface of my emotions. My guess is that everyone in the van was having the same struggle because as we made our way down the highway, no one said a word. The radio was tuned to a Christian music station, and halfway to O'Hare airport, the DJ read the encouraging verse of the day:

> And everyone who has left houses or brothers or sisters or father or mother or children or lands, for My name's sake, will receive a hundredfold and will inherit eternal life. Matthew 19:29

I'm not sure any of us found that verse all that "encouraging" that day. But God knew we needed to hear it. He knew my daughter—who was doing the leaving—needed to hear it. And He knew that I—who was being left behind—

needed to hear it too. God was trying to tell me that in the leaving and in the sacrifice, He would provide for them—and me. Waiting well means letting go and trusting that God will bless us in ways we can't yet imagine.

But even after hearing those words on the radio, even after listening to God's clear nudge to let go—I couldn't do it.

While waiting, the Holy Spirit can give peace.
Hannah experienced an amazing blessing when she praised God as the Lord of hosts and surrendered her heart's desire to Him. We read in 1 Samuel 1:18 that after she had prayed, she "went her way and ate, and her face was no longer sad." This broken-hearted, tortured woman entered the tabernacle court weeping, so upset she couldn't eat the festival meal. She was "deeply distressed" and "wept bitterly" (1 Samuel 1:10). But after she poured out her soul to the Lord, she was no longer depressed and dejected.

But she was still waiting. Hannah had not yet reached the front of the line. She was still yearning for a child. And while Eli's words "Go in peace, and the God of Israel grant your petition that you have made to Him" (1 Samuel 1:17) were encouraging, they were not a sure word of prophecy that her prayers would be answered the way she wanted.

So why was Hannah "no longer sad"? How could she "go in peace"?

Hannah had met with the living God. She knew where to go when her heart was overwhelmed with sorrow. She entered the tabernacle court and opened her heart, placing all her dreams and desires on God's altar. Hannah let go of her desire and received peace even before God gave her what she was waiting for.

When we are sad, discouraged, and distressed, we all have a place to go. God calls us to come to Him—in His Word and at His Table. And as we come to Him with our aching souls, a new intimacy develops. When we entrust our troubles to the Lord of hosts, our relationship with Him deepens.

God promises us that when we release our burdens to Him, we will experience a peace that transcends our circumstances:

> Do not be anxious about anything, but in everything by prayer and supplication with thanksgiving let your requests be made known to God. And the peace of God, which surpasses all understanding, will guard your hearts and your minds in Christ Jesus. Philippians 4:6–7

> Waiting well means letting go and trusting that God will bless us in ways we can't yet imagine.

Hannah experienced this serenity in letting go. Relinquishing our deepest desires to our Lord can generate peace. Surrender can bring a release from the tension of wanting and not having.

But the peace is not simply a by-product of the act of sacrificing our desires. It is the result of placing them in the hands of the One who rules the universe. Hannah laid her longing for a child in the hands of the One who was able to change her situation. The One who was known for His mercy and loving kindness.

Our anxious hearts are stilled when we realize God is in control. If our fate were in the hands of chance, we would have no hope. If it were in the hands of men, we would have reason to be afraid. But when we realize it's in the hands of a loving, omnipotent God, we can have confidence and peace.

While waiting, we can receive the gift of joy. The scene of Hannah giving Samuel to the Lord continues to astound me. For one thing, no tears are mentioned. When I hugged my daughter and son-in-law good-bye at O'Hare, I lost the battle with my tears. I was a blubbering mess as I kissed my grandsons on the cheek. But when Hannah left Samuel at the tabernacle, Scripture does not tell us that she sobbed or wept. Instead Scripture records her beautiful prayer of praise. This prayer is often called "the Magnificat of the Old Testament" because of its similarities to the song Mary sings after Gabriel has told her she would be the mother of the Savior. Hannah prayed:

> My heart exults in the LORD;
> my horn is exalted in the LORD.
> My mouth derides my enemies,
> because I rejoice in Your salvation.
> There is none holy like the LORD:
> for there is none besides You;
> there is no rock like our God.
>
> 1 Samuel 2:1–2

This passage tells us that Hannah exulted. That is not a word we use often. What does it mean to exult? *Exult* is defined as "to show or feel a lively or triumphant joy; rejoice exceedingly; be highly elated or jubilant."[9] Hannah exhibited triumphant joy even as she surrendered what she loved. How was that possible?

It was only possible because Hannah exulted *in the Lord*. Her joy was not found in earthly blessings. Hannah was able to wait well because her contentment was based in her all-powerful and loving God. In her poetic prayer, Hannah says, "there is none besides You" (1 Samuel 2:2). No one else—not even a long-awaited child—came before the Holy God.

Reflecting on that day in Iowa, I'm sure I did not have that same heart attitude. As I stood at the podium, speaking about Christ's love, God needed to interrupt my presentation to shout to my heart, "Sharla, am I not enough for you?"

Clearly, I had been acting as if He wasn't. I pouted that God hadn't come around to my way of thinking. I insisted that I couldn't be happy unless God gave me what I wanted. My daughter had moved halfway around the world—and I wouldn't let her go. My heart held on.

After my presentation, I made my way to the home where I would spend the night and got down on my knees in the privacy of my room. I realized God wanted me to accept my new life—a life that wasn't exactly what I wanted. But I also realized I couldn't honestly do that. I *wanted* to be able to say, "God, You are enough. I will say yes to Your plan for my life and for my daughter's." But on my own, I didn't have the strength to do it.

So I had to ask for God's grace. My prayer went something like this: "Lord, I *want* to say that You are enough for me. I *want* to want Your way. But You know my heart. You know I'm struggling with this. Help me to *want* Your will. Help me to release my desires into Your hands."

That was the start. I can't say I experienced an immediate flood of peace and joy about my situation. Unlike Hannah who went away "no longer sad," my spirit was still heavy. But as I continued to wait, God gradually gave me the grace to accept His plan.

God blessed Hannah for her sacrifice. We learn in 1 Samuel 2 that after Hannah left Samuel in Eli's care, she visited him every year. And every year Eli would bless Elkanah and say, "May the Lord give you children by this woman for the petition she asked of the Lord" (1 Samuel 2:20). And God did bless Hannah with three more sons and two daughters (1 Samuel 2:21).

Unlike Hannah, I did not receive what my heart longed for. My daughter and her family still live in China. I am still in between my petition and the realization of my hope. But as I have stood in line for the answer to that prayer, I have slowly let it go. I have given it over to God to hold, to take care of.

Sometimes the Lord uses long delays in our life plans to wean us from demanding our own way. As we stand in line with the burden of our own

Sometimes the Lord uses long delays in our life plans to wean us from demanding our own way.

will, we slowly become aware of its weight. While we wait to receive our requests from God, we may become impatient and angry. But eventually the millstone of our own self-made agendas becomes so heavy that we release it to God. And when we finally let it go, God lightens our spirit and imparts the gift of His joy.

Be Still

Visiting our daughter in China involves standing in a lot of lines. First, my husband and I queue up at the Chinese consulate in Chicago to obtain our visas. In fact, we usually do this several times for just one visa, because inevitably the rules will have changed and we will be missing an important document.

On the day of our flight, we stand in security lines at O'Hare airport. We wait to get on the plane. We endure a fifteen-hour flight to Beijing, get off, retrieve our luggage, and stand in more lines for Chinese customs and security. We wait at the gate for the flight to the city where our daughter's family lives, and when we arrive, we wait for our bags. Finally, after twenty or more hours of travel, we are able to wrap our arms around our loved ones.

During these journeys, standing in a line is a given. But I have learned through these adventures in waiting that I do have a choice. I can choose to wait in patience or agitation, stillness or anxiety.

We have the same choice in life. Although life without delay is not an option, we can decide how we will wait.

Psalm 37:7 reminds us:

> Be still before the LORD and wait patiently for Him;
> fret not yourself over the one who prospers in his way,
> over the man who carries out evil devices!

We wait well when we follow the psalmist's instructions to "Be still." But how is this quiet possible? This stillness of spirit comes when we have poured out our souls and surrendered all our hopes and dreams to Him. Until then, we will keep striving and conniving and working on our projects. When we are finally still, God can work in our hearts.

What are you waiting for? What deep desire of your heart remains unmet? Perhaps you've been desperately praying for someone to share your life with. Maybe, like Hannah, you are waiting for a child to hold. Or it could be you long to make a difference in the world but have no idea how.

You pour out your heart day by day. But what you hear from heaven is deafening silence. All you can do is wait. The line for what you want seems to have no end. Frustration grows. Impatience joins you in the line.

> You could be like Hannah and relinquish your desire into the loving hands of God.

You could be like me and stubbornly hold on to your desire. You could follow my example and refuse to be happy until you get your way.

Or you could be like Hannah and relinquish your desire into the loving hands of God. The Father is there, waiting to listen to your heart's cries. He knows what is best. He may satisfy your profound longings at the right time. Or He may give you peace and joy in a new and better plan.

Hannah let go of her desire and received peace even before God gave her what she was waiting for. What if, in the waiting, I let go and allow God to hold my dreams?

God's Grace in Hannah's Story

Much of Hannah's story takes place around Old Testament sacrifices. Hannah and her family, along with the rest of the Israelites, were required to offer animals on the altar at the tabernacle to atone for their transgressions. God had prescribed a way for people to be cleansed from sinful deeds through the blood of lambs and goats and calves. It was a very visual and gory way to demonstrate that there was a price to pay for sin.

Because of Jesus, we no longer need to go to the tabernacle with the blood of animals. He laid Himself on the altar. By the power of the Holy Spirit, Christ offered Himself as the perfect sacrifice (Hebrews 9:14). Because of His sacrificial act, we are now able to enter into God's presence and receive His grace.

— · — · — · — · — · -

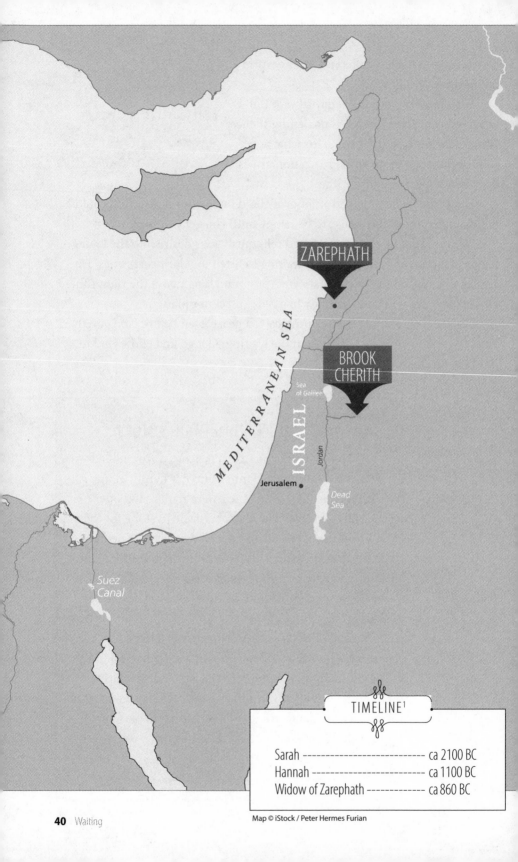

ZAREPHATH

BROOK
CHERITH

MEDITERRANEAN SEA

ISRAEL

*Sea
of Galilee*

Jordan

Jerusalem •

*Dead
Sea*

*Suez
Canal*

TIMELINE[1]

Sarah ---------------------------- ca 2100 BC
Hannah -------------------------- ca 1100 BC
Widow of Zarephath ------------- ca 860 BC

The Widow of Zarephath

Chapter 3

I am a planner and a doer.

I love to make detailed to-do lists, which always include a mix of household chores, writing tasks, and duties for my piano teaching business. And the feeling of triumph I get when checking off a finished task is almost as good as dark-chocolate bliss.

But last year something happened that drastically changed all my to-do lists.

My husband, John, was diagnosed with lymphoma.

To-Do List:
☐ Clean bathrooms
☐ Dust
☐ Vacuum
☐ Go grocery shopping
☐ Order music for piano students
☐ Work on chapter for new book
☐ Wait for PET scan results

Suddenly, my world turned upside down. Pressing to-dos that had been at the top of my list were swiftly bumped to the bottom. Items that had seemed crucial to my schedule were simply forgotten.

Instead, my list looked something like this:

☐ Make appointment with oncologist
☐ Take John to hospital for outpatient surgery
☐ Meet with nurse practitioner to learn how to help John stay healthy during chemotherapy

Oh, and one more thing:
☐ Wait

Anyone who has gone through a health crisis knows that a lot of time is spent waiting. Waiting in hospitals. Waiting for doctors to make rounds. Waiting in pharmacies. Waiting by the phone.

If it were up to me, I would never wait—ever. Yet there have been seasons of my life when God has written "Wait" at the top of my to-do list every day. Unfortunately, during these seasons, I didn't identify waiting as a God-ordained mission. I didn't recognize God's handwriting on the list. So every day I complained. Every day I questioned the value of waiting.

There is a woman in Scripture who also endured a season of waiting—a time in her life when "Wait" was written on her to-do list every day. And her example teaches us how to deal with the daily-ness of waiting.[2]

Prophets of Judah	Kings of Judah	Reigns in Judah (BC)		Reigns in Israel (BC)	Kings of Israel	Prophets of Israel
Shemaiah	Rehoboam	931–914	10th century BC	931–910	Jeroboam	Ahijah
	Abijam	914–911				
Azariah	Asa*	911–870		910–909	Nadab	
Hanani						
Jehu				909–887	Baasha	
			9th century BC	886–885	Elah	
				885	Zimri	
				885–880	Tibni	
				885–874	Omri	
Jahaziel	Jehoshaphat*	873–848		874–853	Ahab	Elijah
Eliezer						Micaiah
				853–852	Ahaziah	Elisha
Obadiah	Jehoram	853–841		852–841	J(eh)oram	
	Ahaziah	841				
Priest Jehoiada	Athaliah	841–835		841–814	Jehu	
Zechariah	Joash*	835–796		814–796	Jehoahaz	
Joel						
	Amaziah	796–767	8th century BC	798–782	Jehoash	Jonah
	Azariah (Uzziah)	792–740		793–753	Jeroboam II	Amos
Isaiah						
Micah	Jotham	750–735		753	Zechariah	
				752	Shallum	
				752–742	Menahem	
				742–732	Pekah	
	Ahaz	735–715		742–740	Pekahiah	Oded
				732–722	Hoshea	Hosea
Nahum	Hezekiah*	715–686		722	Fall of Samaria	
	Manasseh	696–642	7th century BC	The Assyrians deported people from Galilee and Transjordan as early as 733 BC. They crushed Syria in 732 BC. God permitted Assyria finally to destroy idolatrous Israel in 722 BC. Much of the Israelite population was deported and assimilated into upper Mesopotamia (2Ki 15:8–17:23). Assyria resettled other peoples in Israel (2Ki 17:24–41).		
Habakkuk	Amon	642–640				
Zephaniah	Josiah*	640–609				
Huldah						
Jeremiah						
	Jehoahaz	609				
Daniel	Jehoiakim	609–598				
Ezekiel	Jehoiachin	598–597	6th century BC	Nebuchadnezzar became king of Babylon in 605 BC. He deported Jehoiachin of Judah and others in 597 BC (2Ki 24:8–17; 2Ch 36:9–10). More deportations occurred in 587 BC after Jerusalem was destroyed (2Ki 25:1–25; 2Ch 36:11–21). Other Judeans escaped to Egypt after further unrest (2Ki 25:22–26), which resulted in a further deportation c 582 BC. The Judeans lived in refugee colonies in the vicinity of Babylon and were not assimilated. In 539 BC, Cyrus of Persia triumphed over the Babylonians. In 538 BC, he approved the return of the Judeans to their homeland.		
	Zedekiah	597–587				
	Fall of Jerusalem	587				
	Restoration	537 BC				

Setting the Scene

Before I introduce you to this woman, let me give you a little background to the period she lived in. The time is around 874 BC, during the divided kingdom. In the previous chapter, we studied Hannah, who lived during the time of the judges. During her lifetime, the people of Israel began asking for a king, and God instructed Hannah's son, Samuel, to anoint the first two kings—first Saul, then David. During the reigns of Saul and David, the twelve tribes of Israel were united. But after the reign of David's son Solomon, the third king of Israel, the northern tribes rebelled. They broke away from the rest of the kingdom, and from then on, the Northern Kingdom was known as Israel and the Southern Kingdom as Judah.

The Books of 1 and 2 Kings chronicle the reigns of the kings of Israel and Judah. The writer of these books records what each king accomplished and also informs us whether the king "did what was right in the eyes of the LORD" (1 Kings 15:11). Judah had a mixture of both good and bad kings, but all of Israel's kings "did what was evil in the sight of the LORD" (1 Kings 15:34).

Around 874 BC, King Ahab became the ruler of Israel. Not only was he a wicked king, but he "did evil in the sight of the LORD, more than all who were before him" (1 Kings 16:30). Like his predecessors, he, too, abandoned worship of the true God, but he went one step further by marrying Jezebel, daughter of the king of the Sidonians, a people known for their worship of the false gods Ashtoreth and Baal. After Jezebel introduced Baal to Ahab, he built a temple and an altar to this false god in the capital city of Samaria (1 Kings 16:31–32).

It was in this pagan environment of Baal worship that God began to act by sending a prophet. Since the Northern Kingdom had no godly kings, and the priests of Yahweh had fled to the Southern Kingdom where God's temple was, God raised up prophets to speak His Word to the people of Israel.

In 1 Kings 17, the prophet Elijah was thrust into the scene. He went to King Ahab and told him, "As the LORD, the God of Israel, lives, before whom I stand, there shall be neither dew nor rain these years, except by my word" (v. 1). Elijah made it very clear whom he served—Yahweh, not Baal. The true God of Israel. The *living* God, who is sovereign over all the earth.

Elijah announced the divine judgment of a drought. This punishment was especially fitting because Baal was considered the god of rain and fertile crops. By withholding rain, Yahweh demonstrated His power and Baal's ineffectiveness.

Right after Elijah gave Ahab God's message, the Lord told the prophet to hide by the brook Cherith. God informed Elijah that He had ordered the ravens to feed him there. And so, for a time, Elijah hid at this brook east of the Jordan River, drinking its water and eating food delivered by ravens every morning and evening.

The Widow's Story

This is when we are introduced to the woman who exemplifies the dailyness of waiting. We are never told her name. We don't know what she looked like or what kind of home she had or how she became a widow. But God chose to use her to feed His prophet and to teach us about waiting well in trust.

Eventually, the drought affected the brook Cherith where Elijah had been hiding out. God allowed the prophet's source of water to dry up so He could reveal the next part of His plan for spreading His word. He said to Elijah, "Arise, go to Zarephath, which belongs to Sidon, and dwell there. Behold, I have commanded a widow there to feed you" (1 Kings 17:9).

Now, if I had been Elijah, I would have had a few questions for the Lord. "Hey, God, are You sure about this? You want me to go to Zarephath of *Sidon*? The

WHY ZAREPHATH?

Why did God send Elijah to Zarephath? One answer might be found in Jesus' words in the Gospel of Luke: "And He said, 'Truly, I say to you, no prophet is acceptable in his hometown. But in truth, I tell you, there were many widows in Israel in the days of Elijah, when the heavens were shut up three years and six months, and a great famine came over all the land, and Elijah was sent to none of them but only to Zarephath, in the land of Sidon, to a woman who was a widow'" (Luke 4:24–26). Jesus was talking about a prophet not being welcomed in his hometown. Most likely the Israelites were angry with Elijah—blaming him for the drought and their distress. The Lord may have sent Elijah out of Israel for his safety.

Jesus' words angered His audience because they suggested Gentiles would be included in the Messiah's salvation. Elijah's journey to the heart of Baal country may have also been God's method of bringing His message to people outside the nation of Israel. We can only wonder, did the widow of Zarephath become a powerful witness of Yahweh's love and faithfulness to her Baal-worshiping neighbors?

nation where Jezebel is from? They worship Baal there, not You! Isn't there some place in *Israel* I could go? There must be some better alternative. Plus, You have ordered a *widow* to supply me with food? If You haven't noticed, widows in this day and age aren't known for their wealth or stockpiles of food."

But I am not Elijah, of course, and Scripture does not record any questions like that from Elijah. It simply says, "So he arose and went to Zarephath" (1 Kings 17:10). Perhaps the obedient prophet reasoned, *If God can use these crazy ravens to feed me for months, then He can use a poverty-stricken widow to keep me from starving to death.*

When Elijah reached Zarephath (a journey of eighty to one hundred miles), he saw a widow gathering sticks at the city gate. How did he recognize her as a widow? We don't know if she was wearing the clothes of mourning or if God simply revealed to Elijah that this was the woman He had ordained to provide for him.

Elijah asked her, "Would you bring me a little water in a jar so I might have a drink?" The widow willingly went to fetch the water, and Elijah called after her, "Oh, and please bring me a morsel of bread."

The woman was prepared to get the water, but she informed the prophet she had no bread, only a little flour in a jar and a little oil in a jug. "I was only gathering sticks so I could make a little fire and cook a final meal

YAHWEH

When the widow meets Elijah at the city gate, she explains her extreme situation to Elijah, saying, "As the LORD your God lives, I have nothing baked, only a handful of flour in a jar and a little oil in a jug" (1 Kings 17:12). Scholars disagree on whether these words indicate she believed in the true God.

Some say she didn't have true faith because she said "the LORD *your* God" instead of "the LORD *my* God." But others think that because she used the name "LORD," she probably believed in the true God.

In our modern Bible, the name "LORD" in capital letters is a translation of the covenant name God first revealed to Moses in Exodus 3:14–15, I AM WHO I AM. For many years, the Jewish people thought this name was too holy to speak aloud. They began to substitute "the Lord" (in Hebrew, *Adonai*) for God's covenant name. So the pronunciation of the original name was lost. Scholars believe that name was originally Yahweh (pronounced YAH-way). The name emphasizes God's eternal nature and ever-present nearness to His people.[3]

for myself and my son," she replied.

But God answered with a solution, and Elijah shared it with the widow:

> Do not fear; go and do as you have said. But first make me a little cake of it and bring it to me, and afterward make something for yourself and your son. For thus says the LORD, the God of Israel, "The jar of flour shall not be spent, and the jug of oil shall not be empty, until the day that the LORD sends rain upon the earth." 1 Kings 17:13-14

Now, put yourself in the widow's sandals for a moment. What might have been going through her mind? *Do not fear? Who is this man to tell me not to be afraid? It's obvious he's a prophet. And I've heard of his God, Yahweh. It is said He is the one who has caused this drought. People are dying right and left, and my son and I have only a few bites of food until we go to the grave, but I'm supposed to take the last bite of food from my son and give it to a complete stranger?*

Ultimately she decided to take the risk of giving away what she had in order to get more. Perhaps she was responding out of faith in Yahweh. Or possibly she decided to take a chance on Elijah's promise because one last meal for herself and her son would not extend their lives beyond the next day. Maybe she thought, *Better to bet my last meal on the hopes of more than to lose any opportunity for a source of food. Better to grasp at the possibility that the promise of the prophet is true.*

So the woman went home and made a little fire in her oven.

BAKING BREAD

When Elijah met the widow, she was gathering sticks so she could make one last cake of bread for her and her son. Without a modern oven, how did she and other women of the ancient world bake bread?

She might have used a simple camp oven—a circle of sheet iron about 30 inches in diameter. This sheet of metal would have been greased with olive oil and placed over a fire, held above the ground by a circle of stones. Flour mixed with oil was baked into flat cakes of bread, much like our pancakes.

Another type of simple oven was a cylinder of clay approximately 3 feet high and 2 feet in diameter. A fire was built at the bottom of the cylinder and then left to smolder. Small loaves of bread were stuck to the inside of the clay cylinder above the coals and left there to bake.[4]

She dumped the last of the flour into a bowl, poured in the final few drops of oil, stirred it together, and made a little cake. When it was baked, she gave it to Elijah. Did her hands tremble as she handed it to him? Did her son look on hungrily as the prophet ate the last of their food?

And then, the miracle the prophet promised actually happened. After Elijah had eaten, the widow proceeded to use any remaining flour and oil to prepare food for herself and her son, as Elijah said in 1 Kings 17:13. Surely that was the last of her provisions. Surely she and her son, as well as this visiting prophet, had eaten their last meal. But then she looked in the jar and saw more flour! Maybe she shook her jug and heard oil slosh inside, even though she was certain she had used every drop. But . . . no. "She and he and her household ate for many days. The jar of flour was not spent, neither did the jug of oil become empty, according to the word of the LORD that He spoke by Elijah" (1 Kings 17:15–16).

Scripture tells us they ate for many days. How long did Elijah live with this woman? We know the drought lasted for three and a half years. Elijah had lived at the brook Cherith for part of the time, but perhaps he lived with the widow and her son for two years or more. Did Elijah interact with the son who had no father? Did the prophet talk to the widow about the Lord?

We aren't sure about Elijah's interaction with his host family, but we do know that one day, a tragedy happened that dramatically changed the woman's view of the Lord. Her son suddenly became ill. This illness was "so severe that there was no breath left in him" (1 Kings 17:17). And the widow confronted Elijah: "What have you against me, O man of God? You have come to me to bring my sin to remembrance and to cause the death of my son!" (1 Kings 17:18). She equated her agony and suffering at the loss of her son with judgment. She knew the drought was judgment on

UPPER ROOMS

When the widow's son died, Scripture tells us, Elijah carried him to "the upper chamber where he lodged" (1 Kings 17:19). Homes in the area of Palestine usually had flat roofs and often had an upper room built on part of the roof. The stairway to the roof might have been inside the home but was more often on the outside of the structure.[5]

Elijah was not the only prophet to live in an upper room. His successor, Elisha, also lived in an upper room, built especially for him by the wealthy Shunammite woman (2 Kings 4:8–10).

the sin of the Israelite nation, so her conclusion that her loss was judgment on her own sin seemed logical.

Her son's death seemed so unfair. The widow had obeyed God's instructions. She put up with Elijah's invasion of her privacy for months or even years. It was bad enough to experience a drought and watch her neighbors suffer too. But now her son was gone. The son who would have provided for her in her old age had been taken away.

Elijah didn't even address her question about her sin. He simply took the lifeless boy from her arms and carried him to the upper chamber where he had been staying. The prophet stretched himself out on the boy three times and cried out, "O LORD my God, let this child's life come into him again" (1 Kings 17:21).

"The LORD listened to the voice of Elijah. And the life of the child came into him again, and he revived" (1 Kings 17:22). Elijah scooped up the boy and took him back down the stairs and into the house. Can you imagine the mother's joy? Tears turned to laughter. Despair was transformed into joy.

This little group of people in Zarephath witnessed a miracle that had never happened before—God fashioned life where there had been death. The woman who lived in a land where people sometimes worshiped the false god Baal by sacrificing their own children now saw firsthand the power of the true God. This God did not demand the life of her child but restored it. Bible experts may disagree whether the widow of Zarephath believed in the true God before this incident, but now we hear certainty in her words as she tells Elijah, "Now I know that you are a man of God, and that the word of the LORD in your mouth is truth" (1 Kings 17:24).

Waiting in a Time of Drought

What does the story of the widow of Zarephath have to do with waiting?

Both the widow and Elijah were waiting for the drought to end. She may have been waiting for the day when this strange man would move out of her house too. But she was stuck. She couldn't make it rain, and she couldn't kick out the prophet, for then she would lose her food supply.

When we are in a waiting period, we, too, may feel trapped. It is satisfying to write goals and activities on our to-do lists and cross them off once they are accomplished. We feel productive. But there may be times when we're waiting for an answer to our desperate prayer; when the drought seems to have no end and we have no control. We can't check off that period of our lives as finished. And for you other list makers, having an unchecked box on your to-do list can be maddening.

It's as if God has written "Wait" on every single day of the calendar and at the top of every to-do list.

That's what happened to the widow of Zarephath. Every day she emptied the jar and drained the jug. Every day she was forced to wait for more. Every day she may have wondered if this was the last day the miracle would happen. Every day she needed to trust the Lord.

God used the waiting time to teach the widow—and Elijah—daily dependence on Him. The Lord taught dependence on His Word, dependence on His provision, and dependence on His power.

Dependence on God's Word. "The word of the LORD" is a key phrase in 1 Kings 17. The "word of the LORD" comes to Elijah to tell him to hide by the brook Cherith (1 Kings 17:2–5) and to instruct him to go to Zarephath (vv. 8–9). It is mentioned in conjunction with God's promise that the jar of flour and jug of oil would never be empty (1 Kings 17:16). And the widow expresses her faith in "the word of the LORD" when her son is restored to life (1 Kings 17:24).

As far as we know from Scripture, Elijah never questioned the Word of the Lord. He immediately obeyed. Even when "the word of the LORD" seemed unbelievable (*Ravens are going to feed me?*) or illogical (*You want me to go to Jezebel's old neighborhood?*), Elijah "went and did according to the word of the LORD" (1 Kings 17:5). He believed God's Word and obeyed.

And so God also expects us to obey His Word. Even when the Word of the Lord seems unbelievable, like Psalm 37:34: "Wait for the LORD and keep

ZAREPHATH

The name of the town where the widow lived was *Zarephath*, which means "smelting place"— a place to refine metals and fire bricks.[6] Excavations have uncovered evidence that this port city was a manufacturing center for textiles, pottery, and glassware.[7]

Indeed, this was a refining place for both Elijah and the widow. While they waited day by day for God's provision, dependence on their own strength was stripped away.

When God has placed you in a time of waiting, think of it as your Zarephath, a place for refining your faith. Ask God what needs to be filtered out of your life so pure faith and trust are what remain.

His way, and He will exalt you to inherit the land." (*Lord, in this day and age, you get ahead with action, not with waiting.*) Or when His Word seems illogical, like Psalm 27:14: "Wait for the LORD; be strong." (*But God, waiting is hard. I feel weak and helpless.*) If God asks us to wait, the best thing we can do is to ask the Holy Spirit each day to give us enough strength to obey.

The Word of the Lord also gives us hope. Psalm 130:5–6 says:

> I wait for the LORD, my soul waits,
> and in His word I hope;
> my soul waits for the Lord
> more than watchmen for the morning,
> more than watchmen for the morning.

What an exquisite picture of daily waiting. Like a night watchman, the soul is waiting through a period of darkness for the first glimmer of light. The night may seem long to the watchman, but he is sure of one thing—morning will come. In the same way, we can put our hope in God's Word.

We may be experiencing a prolonged darkness, but we can be sure of one thing—God's Word contains all the comfort and strength and power and truth we need to endure it. God's promises of love and hope and faithfulness shine His light into our gloomy circumstances. God's Holy Spirit gives us the faith we need to believe.

Dependence on God's provision. The drought made it impossible for the widow of Zarephath to depend on her own ingenuity or ability to provide for her daily needs and the needs of her son and her guest. She had come to the end of her flour, and the jug of oil was nearly empty. Elijah's promise for an unending supply of oil seemed impossible, but she took the chance that it might be true. And for the rest of the three-and-a-half-year drought, she daily depended on God's miraculous provision.

Elijah had experienced God's unusual provision even before he arrived in Zarephath. God fed Elijah at the brook Cherith by instructing ravens to bring him food. This was remarkable in so many ways. Ravens were unclean birds according to Mosaic Law. Elijah didn't eat them, but it is still surprising that God used unclean animals as a delivery system. Plus, ravens are carrion-eating birds. Normally they would be the scavengers after the feast, not the caterers of the meal. And while ravens probably could find meat from dead animals, where in the world did they find bread every day? Did some poor woman set out bread to cool on her windowsill every day only to have it stolen by the black birds?

God's provision was surprising in Zarephath too. Why send Elijah all the way to the suburb of Sidon instead of to a village nearby? Why direct him to the heart of Baal worship country instead of the land of Israel? Why send the prophet to a poor widow instead of to a wealthy merchant?

It was all so Elijah and the widow could not mistake the Lord's hand. There was simply no other explanation for wild birds bringing bread or for a jar of oil that never ran dry. God was the source of their provision.

When I am in a waiting wilderness, God often brings me to the point where none of my own efforts make any difference. I have no choice but to wait for Him. I can grumble and complain, but God invites me to witness His miraculous provision in big things and small. Waiting can teach me dependence on God. I wait well when I open my eyes to the creative ways He meets my needs.

One more question. Why did God only provide enough for each day? Why did He not let them relax in abundant supply? Or why hadn't He told them beforehand to spend the years before the drought storing up larders of grain, as He directed Joseph to do in Egypt?

Perhaps He wanted the widow to develop the habit of waiting on the Lord. To daily depend on Him for her needs.

God wants all of us to develop the daily habit of waiting on His provision. Our Lord taught us to pray, "Give us this day our daily bread," yet few of us in the Western world know the desperation of going even a day without food. With full refrigerators and stocked pantries, it's easy to take God's care for granted. So the

God wants all of us to develop the daily habit of waiting on His provision.

Lord may work through seasons of delay to foster reliance on His love. He may use times when we feel totally depleted to develop dependence on His nurturing hand.

In the desolation of a waiting wilderness, we can learn that the Lord is also waiting for us, ready to bestow His peace and joy. In the wastelands where our own sufficiency fails, He waits for His baptized daughters to come to Him in repentance to receive daily grace. In the desert of our disappointments, He daily supplies the oil of patience and the bread of strength.

Dependence on His power. No rain for three-plus years was a disaster on a regional scale. But the widow experienced an extremely personal tragedy in addition to the drought—not only had she previously lost her husband, but now her only son suddenly died. When the prophet entered the room and saw her holding the lifeless body, did she have any inkling that the power of his God was big enough to overcome death? When Elijah took the boy from her arms, did she have a glimmer of hope for another miracle?

Why did the Lord allow tragedy upon tragedy? Not to punish the woman for her sin, as she expressed in 1 Kings 17:18, but to demonstrate His power. Often, when we are in our own seasons of drought, waiting for God to answer our prayers according to our plans, we may also think He is punishing us. Scripture tells us how to get past this.

In the New Testament, the disciples asked Jesus about a blind man they saw on the street: "Rabbi, who sinned, this man or his parents, that he was born blind?" (John 9:2). And Jesus answered, "It was not that this man sinned, or his parents, but that the works of God might be displayed in him" (v. 3). The blindness was not a punishment for sin but an opportunity for God the Son to display His power to heal. In the same way, the tragedy of her son's death gave the widow of Zarephath an opportunity to witness God's life-giving power.

When we're in a waiting place and it seems like tragedies are piling up, we all ask, why? We want answers to the pain and heartache. And yes, God may be using circumstances to point out behaviors or attitudes He wants to change. In that case, we need to repent of our sin and receive Christ's forgiveness.

But maybe the better question to ask is, who? Who has promised to walk with us on this bumpy life path? Who has the power to resolve the situation? Who gives hope when the jar of hope is nearly empty? Who supplies the promise of eternal joy when our circumstances remain broken and bleak? My perspective is changed when I stop searching for a cause, a rationale to my anguish. My hope is renewed when I start anticipating that God will step in and display His power—improving my circumstances or transforming my heart.

Waiting gives us an opportunity to sit back and watch God display His competence. His capability. His invincibility.

When things are moving smoothly in the direction of my plans, I am tempted to become confident in my own abilities. It is then when God may write the word *wait* on my to-do list. Waiting makes me feel powerless. Waiting exposes my limitations.

Waiting gives me an opportunity to sit back and watch God display His competence. His capability. His invincibility.

Learning to wait well starts with the acknowledgment of our impotence and the recognition of God's strength.

Waiting Day by Day

A crash course in waiting began the day we received the news.

It was around 8:00 a.m. I remember I was making a cup of tea in the kitchen when the phone rang. The voice on the other end of the line was our family physician. "Hi, Sharla, this is Dr. Love. Is John there?"

Knowing Dr. Love (don't you *love* his name?) was probably calling with the results of John's biopsy, I quickly ran upstairs to find my husband. My heart raced a little more than usual as I sprinted up the stairs. But as I handed over the phone, I tried to remain calm. Leaving the room to give John privacy, I hung on to Dr. Love's original assessment that the lump on John's neck was nothing more than a lipoma—a benign tumor.

But when I returned to our bedroom, cup of tea in hand, I knew the news was more serious. Instead of a smile, John's face held an expression of stunned numbness. "They think it's lymphoma," he said.

I replied, "Okay. Now I'm worried."

That day launched an intense seminar in waiting. Waiting in doctor's offices. Waiting for test results. Waiting for medicine to drip into John's veins and do its job in annihilating the cancer cells.

Waiting for God to answer our prayers for healing.

At the same time John was diagnosed with lymphoma, my friend Amy was also in the fight of her life against lung cancer. She had been diagnosed four months before John received news of his illness. She was enduring debilitating chemotherapy and radiation treatments. But when I went to visit her, she and her husband remained upbeat. Her husband said their secret weapon was to live one day at a time. I'll never forget his words: "I have Amy today, and for that I am grateful."

This couple was an inspiration to me. And so, like the widow of Zarephath, I began to trust God for the courage to live one day at a time. Some of those days were spent sitting with my husband at the hospital as he received treatments. Some were spent helping him at home when those same treatments zapped every ounce of his strength. And some days—when he felt more like his usual self—were spent doing something "normal" like going to a movie.

Like Amy's husband, I learned to be grateful for each day. I thanked God when I saw His hand at work. Our heavenly Father provided for us through our medical insurance, which covered most of John's medical bills. Our church helped us pay for some of our out-of-pocket expenses. Readers of my newsletter and followers on my social media sites prayed for us. People shared their own positive stories of triumphantly battling cancer.

God supported me through other people in surprising ways. One day when I needed to do a little shopping, I headed to the mall for a few clothing necessities. When I brought my purchases to the cashier, I found myself face-to-face with Bea—a longtime friend and mentor. We hadn't seen each other in a couple of years, but this seemed like a God-ordained meeting. She was shocked to hear of John's illness and promised to call me. A few days later, we met for lunch. God knew I needed Bea's encouragement, and He provided it through a chance meeting. Bea's positive words and fervent prayers lifted my spirits.

God also used this time to winnow my doing. I have already described my fondness for detailed to-do lists, which always became impossibly long. So when crisis struck our family, I realized I would not be able to keep up my usual pace *and* take care of my husband. Not that my usual pace was one I could maintain even before John's diagnosis—I had said yes to too many organizations and too many activities. I perpetually added more to-dos than I could accomplish. My usual pace was characterized by stress and distraction.

To remedy this condition, I used my daily devotion time with the Lord to help me discern what needed to be done and what could be left undone. Each day I would pray and ask God, "What is the *one* thing You want me to do today?" Sometimes my heavenly Father would guide me to a task on my still-too-long list, but often the item He asked me to accomplish was something not even on the list. (Hmm. Maybe that tells me something about my list.) Perhaps the Word would remind me to honor my husband and my one thing that day was spending extra time with John. Or maybe the Holy Spirit would bring to mind a hurting friend and the most pressing task that day was sending her a card. Focusing on finishing that one act each day helped me to not stress out about the other things that were not getting done. Day by day I was doing what I felt was God-pleasing and important. And that was enough.

Thankfully, after six months of chemotherapy, John's cancer was officially in remission. The doctors told John that if he had to get cancer, lymphoma was definitely the kind to get. Did John feel lucky? Uh, I would have to say no. But we do feel extraordinarily blessed and grateful that God has restored John to health. And I'm thankful that God used the crisis to teach me the lesson of living day by day.

Jesus talked about living one day at a time in His Sermon on the Mount:

> "Therefore do not be anxious about tomorrow, for tomorrow will be anxious for itself. Sufficient for the day is its own trouble." M a t t h e w 6 : 3 4

When God has enrolled us in a course on waiting, we feel stuck. We can't make plans for the future because we don't know what the future holds. We don't know what steps to take because the Lord hasn't revealed them yet.

But delay can be God's tool to teach us to wait well. In the book *Waiting on God*, South African pastor Andrew Murray wrote:

> Blessed waiting must and can be the very breath of our life—a continuous resting in God's presence and His love, an unceasing yielding of ourselves for Him to perfect His work in us.[8]

We may be frustrated, angry even, that there seems to be nothing we can do to fix our situation, but in this time of inaction, God is giving us an opportunity to be still in His care. Each day of waiting is another twenty-four hours to watch Him provide for us in miraculous ways. Every pause in our plans is a new chance to relinquish our stubborn hold on our lives and yield to the Lord's perfect will.

The prophet Hosea urges:

> So you, by the help of your God, return,
> hold fast to love and justice,
> and wait continually for your God.
>
> Hosea 12:6

The prophet urges us to "wait continually"—to develop a *habit* of waiting well. Daily depending on God's Word for guidance. Daily waiting on the Lord's provision. Daily resting in His love. But we cannot even do this without the "help of [our] God." The Holy Spirit is the one who gives us the endurance and patience we need each day. Every hour He bids us to return our thoughts to our loving Savior and His forgiveness. Every minute He draws us back to our powerful Father and gives us the strength and courage to wait continually.

Recognize the Lord's handwriting on your to-do list and know the task of waiting can be a God-ordained mission for your life.

What does your to-do list look like? Has God seemingly written "Wait" on every day of your calendar? Recognize His handwriting on the list and know this task of waiting can be a God-ordained mission for your life. Ask the Holy Spirit to help you develop the daily habit of waiting. Use this opportunity to learn to depend on God's Word, God's provision, and God's power.

I don't know about you, but I'm making "Wait" a permanent line item on my list of tasks. Although I used to consider waiting a waste of time and an unnecessary frustration, the Spirit has taught me through a series of very tough lessons that waiting on God is the most important thing I can do each day.

To-Do List:

- ☑ Clean bathrooms
- ☑ Dust
- ☑ Vacuum
- ☑ Go grocery shopping
- ☑ Order music for piano students
- ☑ Work on chapter for new book
- ☑ Wait for PET scan results

God's Grace in the Widow's Story

As a destitute widow living in a center of Baal worship, the widow of Zarephath was an unlikely character in God's story of faith. Yet the Lord used this woman—even though she was poor. Even though she was not part of the nation of Israel.

God chooses to use us too—not because we are important or prominent people. Not because we are wealthy or gifted or talented. Not because we ourselves have something valuable to share.

The Father chooses us simply because He loves us. He accepts us as His own because of Jesus' saving work on the cross. We have value because He has wrapped us in His robes of righteousness. And He uses us as we learn to wait on Him. As we depend on Him for His daily supply of grace to share with the spiritually starving people in our world.

—·—·—·—·—·—

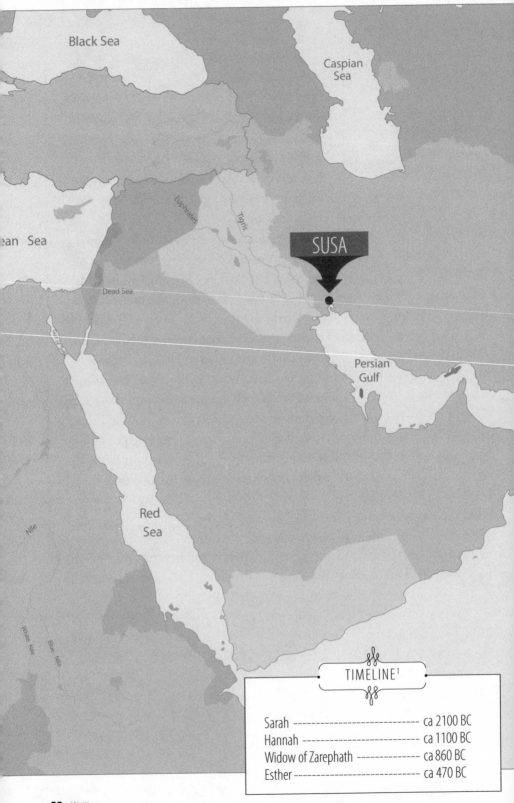

Black Sea

Caspian
Sea

ean Sea

Euphrates

Tigris

SUSA

Dead Sea

Gulf of Suez

Persian
Gulf

Nile

Red
Sea

White Nile

Blue Nile

TIMELINE[1]

Sarah ------------------------- ca 2100 BC
Hannah ------------------------ ca 1100 BC
Widow of Zarephath ------------ ca 860 BC
Esther ------------------------- ca 470 BC

When Waiting Doesn't Mean Doing Nothing

Once upon a time, I was Queen Esther.

To be more exact, I played the part of Queen Esther in a musical. You see, the year after I graduated from high school, I performed with Joy Inc., a Christian group that gave concerts for churches and staged musicals for Sunday Schools.

Our group toured the country in a converted school bus named Miracle White (more about that "miraculous" bus later). We experienced plenty of excitement during our travels.

But we experienced plenty of waiting too.

For me, the adventure of travel is always accompanied by the boredom of killing time. I rush to the airport just to stand in long lines to get through security. I hurry to get the bags stowed in the trunk of my car only to find traffic at a standstill.

We would all prefer no delays in our travels. PLEASE, get me to my destination where I can view awesome scenery, relax on the beach, ride the roller coaster. Anything but these frustrating long layovers and maddening traffic jams where I can do—nothing.

Of course, we also hope for no delays in our life journeys. We don't pray for setbacks in our plans. We don't wish for extended waiting periods where there is nothing to do but sit on our hands, longing for things to change.

Queen Esther and her people experienced delays and setbacks. Frustrating times when things seemed hopeless and time appeared to move in slow motion. But we see in Esther's story that even when we are experiencing a pause in our plans, there are steps we can take and choices we can make.

Setting the Scene

The Book of Esther opens in the city of Susa in the land of Persia. Why Persia? Because that's where Esther and many other Jews were living in 483 BC.

In the last chapter, we met the widow of Zarephath, who lived in the time of Israel's divided kingdom. We learned about King Ahab—a wicked king in a long line of wicked kings of the Northern Kingdom. Because of the evil in the land, God declared judgment on the nation, allowing Assyria to defeat Samaria, the capital of Israel. Shalmaneser, king of Assyria, captured many citizens of Israel and carried them off to Assyria in the year 722 BC.

Significant Events Leading up to Esther	
722 BC	Israel led into captivity
605 BC	Jews like Daniel are taken to Babylon
588 BC	Siege of Jerusalem—more Jews taken to Babylon
537 BC	Some exiles return to Jerusalem
483 BC	Queen Vashti deposed
478 BC	Esther becomes queen

The Southern Kingdom of Judah continued. Good kings like Hezekiah and Josiah renewed the nation's worship of the true God. But eventually Judah also strayed from the Lord and rejected the words of prophets like Isaiah and Jeremiah. God brought judgment through Nebuchadnezzar, king of Babylon, who invaded Judah. Beginning in the year 605 BC, Nebuchadnezzar began deporting Jews to his land, and by 586 BC, he had completely defeated Jerusalem and relocated many of its most distinguished citizens to Babylon.

A few years later, in 538 BC, mighty Babylon was captured by Cyrus, the founder of the Persian Empire. While he allowed many Jews to return to their homeland, many of the people of Israel chose to remain in Persia because they had experienced prosperity in Persia and didn't want to undertake the arduous journey to Zion.[2]

Esther was one of those Jews who chose to stay. Because she was an orphan, her older cousin Mordecai, who had also chosen to stay, adopted her and took her into his home. They lived in the city of Susa, the winter residence of King Ahasuerus (also known by his Greek name, Xerxes).

Party of the Century

Esther's story in Scripture opens on the party of the century in the year 483 BC. King Ahasuerus was preparing for battle with Greece. He was determined to avenge the defeat his father, Darius, had experienced against the Greeks, and so he invited all the nobles and military leaders of the land to a six-month-long gala to convince them to join him in battle.[3] For 180 days, the king showed off "the riches of his royal glory and the splendor and pomp of his greatness" (Esther 1:4). And as if that wasn't enough, the six-month feast was followed by a seven-day party for all the people in Susa. Party decorations included white cotton curtains and purple hangings fastened to silver rods and marble pillars. Drinks were served in golden goblets. Wine flowed freely. The king gave only one order for the event: everyone was to drink as much as they desired.

In the meantime, the queen of the land, Queen Vashti, had been entertaining the women in another part of the palace. But on the seventh day, after King Ahasuerus, together with all of his guests, had been drinking for a week straight, the Bible tells us, "the heart of the king was merry with wine" (Esther 1:10). (That might be a bit of an understatement.) Ahasuerus, in his inebriated state, decided he wanted to see his queen and ordered her to make a royal appearance. Apparently he not only wanted to show off his wealth and splendor, but also his eye candy.

Vashti refused.

Ahasuerus was livid. There he was, trying to display his strength and power to convince his nobles to join him in a risky war maneuver, and he couldn't even control his wife. The king's advisers suggested he make a new law: Queen Vashti must never enter the king's presence again. Her position must be given to someone else. Ahasuerus agreed.

A Beauty Contest

Later on, Ahasuerus's anger simmered down and he remembered his lovely queen. Perhaps he regretted dismissing her. The court attendants devised a plan that was sure to please the king. They explained, "Let beautiful young virgins be sought out for the king. . . . Let their cosmetics be given them. And let the young woman who pleases the king be queen instead of Vashti" (Esther 2:2–4). Surprise, surprise—the king liked this idea.

Well, it turned out that an orphaned Jew named Hadassah had the face and figure of a Persian supermodel. She was taken to the palace, where she underwent a year of waiting through extensive beauty treatments before she met King Ahasuerus. Hegai, the king's eunuch, immediately saw this young woman's potential and gave her the best place in the harem. He assigned seven ladies-in-waiting to help her prepare for her meeting with the king. All the while, Hadassah did not reveal her nationality because Mordecai had advised her to wait.

After twelve months of myrrh and spice cosmetic treatments, it was finally her turn to meet the king. She would meet him as Esther—her Persian name—so as not to betray her true nationality. Ahasuerus was immediately taken with her and announced Esther had won the beauty contest. She received the crown and became queen.

ESTHER/HADASSAH

It was not uncommon for the exiled Jews to have both a Hebrew and a Persian name. The heroine of our story was known by her Hebrew name, *Hadassah*, which meant "myrtle," and her Persian name, *Esther*, which meant "star." An interesting point is that in Hebrew, the name *Esther* has the verbal root of *str*, which means "to conceal." God's hiddenness is a primary theme in the Book of Esther.[4]

Mordecai and His Archenemy

Meanwhile, Esther's cousin had been busy. Esther 2:21 tells us Mordecai sat at the king's gate, and because that's where all the official business of Susa took place, we surmise that Mordecai held a government position. One day, while at the gate, Mordecai overheard a plot to murder the king. He informed Esther of the conspiracy, and she passed the information to the king. An investigation was conducted and the two men involved in the plot were executed.

But while Mordecai was hanging out at the king's gate, he also encountered King Ahasuerus's new top man—Haman. The king decreed that everyone bow to Haman because he was second in command. All the officials obeyed and paid homage—all except Mordecai. His refusal to pay homage infuriated Haman, and when he discovered Mordecai was a Jew, he decided that punishing only Mordecai was not enough. He determined to annihilate all the Jews in Persia, and he obtained the king's permission to declare their destruction. Lots were cast to establish the date of the massacre, and a date almost twelve months from the signing of the decree was chosen. More waiting.

When Mordecai found out the news, he told Esther she would have to go to the king and plead for her people. Esther wasn't against going to see the king. But she told her cousin that there was one little problem: anyone who entered the king's court without being summoned would be put to death—unless the king held out his golden scepter. And, well, Ahasuerus had not called for her for thirty days. It wasn't likely she'd be summoned anytime soon.

Mordecai reminded Esther that she was a Jew and, although no one in the court knew her secret, she could not stand idly by as her people were destroyed. He then asked the famous question: "Who knows whether you have not come to the kingdom for such a time as this?" (Esther 4:14).

Esther didn't immediately go to the king—she waited. She relayed a message to Mordecai to have all the Jews fast for three days on her behalf. She told him that she and her ladies-in-waiting would do the same and that on the third day, she would go to the king. She ended her message with the words "and if I perish, I perish" (Esther 4:16).

HAMAN THE AGAGITE

The bad guy of the story is introduced in Esther 3:1 as Haman the Agagite. It is thought the term *Agagite* means Haman was a descendant of the Amalekite king Agag, an ancient enemy of King Saul of Israel. The Lord declared continual hostility between the Israelites and Amalekites in Exodus 17:8–15. The animosity between Haman and Mordecai could have been based in the age-old enmity between the Amalekites and Jews. Mordecai may have refused to bow to Haman because of his ancestry.[5]

On the third day, Esther put on her royal robes. (I wonder if she had trouble deciding what to wear. *Should I wear the azure blue robe because it's the most flattering? Or the scarlet because that's the king's favorite?*) She walked from her quarters to the inner court of the king's palace. (Were her knees shaking? her palms sweaty? Was her heart pounding?) Entering the inner court, she raised her eyes to her husband's throne elevated on a series of steps. (Did he notice her right away? Or was he deep in discussion over national matters when one of the courtiers announced, "Queen Esther!"?) Time must have stood still as Esther held her breath and waited. Can you imagine the thoughts circling in her head? *Will I be banished like Vashti? Will I be executed? Or will he summon me to come forward?*

Esther finally exhaled when the king extended the golden scepter.

She gratefully stepped forward and touched the tip of the scepter. Ahasuerus realized the queen probably had not risked death to simply say hello. He asked, "What is it, Queen Esther? What is your request? It shall be given you, even to the half of my kingdom" (Esther 5:3).

Esther could not have hoped for a more favorable opportunity. But instead of immediately blurting out her request, she chose to wait. (What? *Chose* to wait?) She told Ahasuerus, "If it please the king, let the king and Haman come today to a feast that I have prepared for the king" (Esther 5:4). Ah, maybe even in 480 BC she knew the familiar adage "The way to a man's heart is through his stomach."

Ahasuerus and Haman came to the queen's feast, and when the king's tummy was full and he was enjoying his after-dinner drink, he repeated his question: "What is your wish, Queen Esther?"

But once again, Esther *waited*. She told the king, "My wish is: If I have found favor with the king, may he and Haman come to another feast tomorrow." If I were the king, I would have said, "Esther, why are you waiting? Just tell me what you want!"

But a lot happened before the second feast. First, Haman got a big head—he bragged to his friends and family that he was invited to dinner with the

CHIASTIC STRUCTURE IN ESTHER

Many commentators talk about the chiastic structure of the Book of Esther. A chiasm is a literary device where events or ideas are presented and then repeated in reverse order. The elements of the items on either side of the turning point are related in subject matter. The term comes from the Greek letter *chi*, which looks like our letter *X*.

Here is one way to look at the chiastic structure of Esther.

Two feasts of Ahasuerus

Esther made queen—conceals her nationality

Haman is made second in command

Mordecai discovers Haman's plot

Esther's first banquet

The king's sleepless night

Esther's second banquet

Esther reveals Haman's plot

Haman is hanged

Esther reveals her nationality and saves her people

Two feasts of Purim

Chiastic structure is interesting, but the point of this structure in the Book of Esther is God's reversal of events, starting with the king's sleepless night. Just when all hope is lost for the Jews, Ahasuerus happens to ask for his book of records, and suddenly God changes the destiny of His people.

queen and that everything would be perfect if he just didn't have to put up with that insubordinate Mordecai. His friends urged him to erect a gallows seventy-five feet high and hang Mordecai immediately. Haman was tickled with this idea.

However, before Haman was able to finish the deed, Ahasuerus was lying restlessly in his palace, unable to sleep. Maybe he was wondering what his beautiful queen was up to. Maybe he simply had too much for dinner. Since Tylenol PM wasn't available, he asked for the next best thing—a history book. The book of records was brought to the king's quarters. Yawn-inducing accounts of crops and taxes would do the trick. But instead, the story the attendant turned to was the thrilling account of Mordecai foiling the assassination plot against the king. When Ahasuerus found out nothing had been done to reward Mordecai, he asked his right-hand man, Haman,

"What should be done to reward the man the king wishes to honor?" Haman, assuming he himself was the one about to be honored, told the king, "Clothe him in royal robes, set a crown on his head, and let him ride on the king's horse." But much to Haman's dismay, it was Mordecai who got the royal treatment. Instead of leading Mordecai to the gallows, Haman was ordered to lead his archenemy through the streets of Susa, yelling, "This is what is done for the man the king desires to honor!"

After Mordecai's honor parade, Haman hurried to the queen's palace for the second banquet. And after the king had eaten his fill, he again asked Esther, "What is your wish?"

Esther finally told the king her request: "If it please the king, let my life be granted. For we have been sold, I and my people, to be destroyed and annihilated."

The king shouted, "Who has dared to do this?"

Esther pointed to Haman. "A foe and enemy! This wicked Haman!" (Esther 7:6).

Ahasuerus, beside himself with anger, marched out of the room, into the palace garden. Haman seized the moment to beg for his life and fell on the queen's couch—just in time for the king to come back into the room. Haman's groveling for mercy was perceived as an assault on Esther, and a livid Ahasuerus commanded Haman be hung on the gallows he had constructed for Mordecai.

Whew! The bad guy was taken care of. Esther then revealed her relationship to Mordecai, and Mordecai was elevated to Haman's old position. But there was still one little problem—the edict declaring that all Jews be killed on the thirteenth day of the twelfth month. And all the laws of the Medes and Persians had one thing in common: they could not be rescinded.

Although they could not change Haman's law, Ahasuerus authorized Esther and Mordecai to send out another royal decree, this one allowing the Jews to defend themselves. And on that fateful day in the twelfth month, the Jews were victorious over their enemies.

Waiting with Nothing to Do

The year I acted the part of Queen Esther, I experienced a painful waiting period. Of course, I had a blast playing the part of the queen. I adored wearing the royal gown (even if it was the old prom dress of another member of the group). I enjoyed the comic scene of the messenger running back and forth between Queen Esther and Mordecai when the older cousin is revealing Haman's plot. And I loved the climax of the musical when I got to stand up, point at Haman, and declare, "It is him! The enemy is Haman!"

But I did not love the waiting period that was imposed on our group when our bus, trusty old Miracle White, broke down in the Mojave Desert in California. It happened in the middle of the night as we were driving from Los Angeles to Colorado, rushing to get to our next concert. Bill was at the wheel, but most of us were asleep when the old converted school bus complained in one deafening *ker-chunk* and came to a sudden stop. Bill hitchhiked into the nearest town and came back with a tow truck emblazoned with the logo of Death Valley Towing. (Not terribly encouraging.) We spent the rest of that night in a hotel that wouldn't earn even a one-star rating on TripAdvisor. I don't think any of us slept, even though the roaches had kindly moved over enough to let us get to the beds. The next night was spent on the floor of a church that graciously let us crash there. But when it was discovered Miracle White's engine had thrown a rod and would need two weeks' repair time, we knew that wasn't a long-term solution.

Our group's leader called a church youth director he knew who was located in nearby Las Vegas. After hearing about our situation, the youth director organized a caravan of vehicles to pick us up, and he convinced enough people in his church to house some Christian vagabonds for the interminably long two weeks of waiting for the bus to be fixed. I am forever grateful to the people who took us in, but the time of delay was excruciating. Concerts were canceled—we couldn't perform. Our musical equipment was stored—we couldn't practice. Our group members were staying in homes scattered throughout the city—we couldn't easily get together.

What do you do when there is nothing to do? Perhaps the most frustrating aspect of this kind of waiting is that we're stuck in a place where we can't fix the situation on our own or carry out a solution. Give me action points to get the desired outcome. Show me a timeline on a calendar. Outline seven steps that will accomplish my plan (or twenty or even a hundred). Just don't ask me to wait.

So what do you do when waiting has put your life on hold? Whether you're waiting for weeks for a temporary situation to be resolved or figuratively holding your breath for years, anticipating a crucial resolution of your circumstances, Esther's example gives us an answer—PRAY. Okay, I know this sounds like a cliché, but bear with me. The word *PRAY* stands for four things we can do in a season of waiting. Esther shows us that even when there seems to be nothing we can do, we have choices to make. We can choose to **P**repare for what is coming, **R**est in God's providence, **A**sk God for the next step, and **Y**ield to God's sovereignty.

Prepare for What Is Coming. Esther's story starts out like an episode of *The Bachelor*: Many beautiful young women are vying to marry one handsome man. Contestants have access to luxurious cosmetics and elegant clothing. Winner takes all. (However, in 480 BC, the prize was not a rose or even a glittering diamond engagement ring. It was a royal crown.)

On the surface, it sounds like a fairy tale come true: an ordinary girl becomes queen of Persia. But with Esther's royal digs came a long wait. She had twelve months of beauty treatments before she even saw the king! While most of us would welcome a little pampering, imagine a *year* of waiting with Oil of Olay on your face, wondering, *Will I be chosen to marry this powerful man? Will I become queen of the land? Or will I become just another one-night stand before being relegated to the harem?*

Esther could have been bitter. She didn't sign up for this beauty contest. When the edict went out that all the beautiful young virgins of the land be brought to the harem, Esther "was *taken* into the king's palace and put in *custody* of Hegai, who had charge of the women" (Esther 2:8, emphasis added). Perhaps she was excited at first, but when she realized she would have to give up her family and Jewish heritage, anger could have bubbled up.

Or Esther could have responded with resignation. She could have spent the year pouting. She could have thrown up her hands and decided there was

> ## THE BACHELOR— PERSIA EDITION
>
> The beauty contest in the Book of Esther sounds like a season of *The Bachelor*: one handsome man choosing from a bevy of beauties.
>
> There was one important difference: the women on *The Bachelor* opt to be on the show, but Esther and the other young women in Persia probably had no choice in the matter. While they doubtless enjoyed many luxuries they otherwise would not have had, this was a permanent assignment.
>
> One of the young women would become queen, but all the others simply became part of the king's harem. After a night with the king, a girl gained prestige as a sexual partner who was provided for, but she had no legal rights as a spouse. As a member of the harem, she gave up her independence, most likely never leaving the palace. She lost contact with her family and forfeited the chance to have a normal family of her own. And as if this were not enough of a sacrifice, the woman might never see the king again, unless he asked for her by name.

little she could do to make the king choose her out of the hundreds of other beautiful girls. She could have thought, *Why even make any effort?*

But instead, Esther used the waiting time to her advantage. She prepared for what was ahead. Like all the other girls, she went through the required beauty treatments and studied the etiquette of the court. But there was something different about Esther. Right from the start, Hegai, the man in charge of these women, saw Esther's beauty and gave her the best place in the harem. Esther 2:15 tells us, "Esther was winning favor in the eyes of all who saw her." She prepared for what was ahead by accepting her place of waiting.

Esther also prepared for what was ahead by learning from the expert. As each girl took her turn to go to the king, she had the opportunity to take whatever she wanted from the harem to the palace. She could choose the most elaborate gown and the most extravagant jewelry. But Esther let Hegai choose for her. After all, he would know if the king liked red silk better than blue satin. Or emeralds better than diamonds. Or Chanel No. 5 better than Shalimar. She didn't proudly insist on her own preferences but deferred to someone who could make the best choice. In humility, she prepared for what was coming by learning from someone else's experience.

How can you use your waiting time to prepare for what is coming? Perhaps you are waiting for a new job. While you are waiting, can you expand your knowledge in your field or improve your interviewing skills? Can you take advantage of community programs or your local library's resources? Or maybe you've been asking God for a friend. You could use the waiting time to study what the Bible says about being a good friend. You could even get involved in a small group at church or a volunteer organization that would give you the chance to meet new friends.

When my touring group was forced to wait, we prepared for what was next by finding opportunities to perform at churches and organizations in the Las Vegas area. Although our equipment was in storage, we had a small repertoire of acoustic and a cappella numbers. We kept up our skills and found ways to connect with people we never would have met without the long delay.

Rest in God's Providence. There is a lot of waiting in the story of Esther.

1. Esther waited to reveal her nationality.
2. Mordecai waited for his reward for thwarting the assassination plot.
3. Esther waited three days to go to the king.
4. She waited to state her request.
5. The Jews waited almost a year for the date of their proposed destruction.

And yet, when we come to the end of the story, we learn of God's perfect timing. Although God's name is never used, we can see Him working behind the scenes throughout Esther's story. There are too many coincidences to be—well, coincidental. The casting of lots set the date for the destruction of the Jews almost a year in advance—giving the Jews added time to prepare to defend themselves. Mordecai was not rewarded for exposing the assassination plot until the night before Esther revealed Haman's scheme—putting the king in a favorable opinion toward Mordecai's race. Haman built a gallows for Mordecai—providing Ahasuerus with a convenient place to execute the man who wanted to destroy his wife and her people. The entire Book of Esther is a testimony to God's providence.

While our musical group had our unexpected layover in Las Vegas, our director was back in our headquarters in Milwaukee rearranging our itinerary. Yes, we had to cancel two weeks' worth

WHERE IS GOD IN ESTHER?

Look for God's name in Esther and you won't find it—not even once. Why this curious omission in a book of Scripture?

Perhaps the author purposely chose (under inspiration) this method of unfolding the narrative to underline the fact that God works in hidden ways. Even when we can't see Him acting, He is in control of events backstage, behind the curtain of the visible world.

This technique emphasizes the providence of God—the unceasing activity of God to govern the universe. In His love, He continually guides and directs the world of men.

of performances. But when Miracle White was finally rolling again, we embarked on a whole new series of concerts in New England and Canada. As a group member, I didn't see any of the booking process; I simply trusted that our director would orchestrate the best possible schedule.

Sometimes life seems as if we are on an incredible journey—and then suddenly, the bus breaks down. We feel trapped in a desert of delay with no way to move on. And in the in-between, it seems God isn't doing anything to fix our situation. We're tempted to complain and pout. To grumble and grow bitter.

That's when we need to remember the story of Esther and how God worked behind the scenes to rescue her people. We wait well when we remind ourselves that even while we're waiting, our Lord is paving the way ahead, scheduling exciting experiences, and booking new destinations for our lives. That's when we need to *choose* to rest in God's providence.

Ask God for the next step. When Mordecai informed Esther of the impending crisis, she could have responded immediately. The situation was dire. Mordecai emphasized the fact that her response was crucial. But Esther chose to wait.

Esther told her cousin, "Go, gather all the Jews to be found in Susa, and hold a fast on my behalf, and do not eat or drink for three days, night or day. I and my young women will also fast as you do. Then I will go to the king" (Esther 4:16). In Scripture, fasting normally included prayer, so although prayer is not specifically mentioned, we can assume Esther was asking the Jews to pray for divine deliverance. She purposely waited three days, using the time to seek God's wisdom and His saving hand.

> While we're waiting, our Lord is paving the way ahead, scheduling exciting experiences, and booking new destinations for our lives.

Esther's example demonstrates that a period of waiting—whether short or excruciatingly long—can actually be a blessing. Although we grumble about any postponements in our self-defined goals and objectives, a delay can be a time to approach God in prayer. To intercede for others. To ask Him to reveal our next steps. And to plead for the courage to take that step.

Proceeding without prayer can be disastrous. I should know. How many times have I proceeded with my plans on the advice of experts instead of the counsel of the Holy Spirit? How many times have I neglected to take the time to seek God's will only to fall on my face?

A time of waiting may be necessary. In some seasons of our lives, the delay will be imposed on us and we can thank God for the pause in which we can pray, read His Word, and determine His will for our lives before moving ahead. Other times, like Esther, we may *choose* to wait before stepping out in a new venture or opportunity—praying that God reveals *His* itinerary for our lives.

Back in Las Vegas, our group was facing a crisis. As you can imagine, rebuilding Miracle White's engine cost a bit more than filling the gas tank. And our shrunken concert schedule meant we weren't bringing in any revenue. All of this weighed on my mind and made me question, why had God allowed this breakdown? I spent a lot of the waiting time in Las Vegas in prayer, asking God to reveal any problems in our group. God led me to the passage about the armor of God in Ephesians 6. Sadly, I and many in our group saw we had let the breastplate of righteousness slip (Ephesians 6:14). We all wrestled with the next step. For some members, that next move meant

> Sometimes it takes an enforced waiting period for us to take the time to seek God's will.

leaving the group. For others, it meant repenting, asking for God's forgiveness, and moving forward. Neither step was easy.

Sometimes it takes an enforced waiting period for us to take the time to seek God's will.

Yield to God's Sovereignty. After fasting for three days, Esther made her way to the king's palace. I wonder if her legs felt shaky from hunger and fear or if she strode toward the palace in supernatural, God-given strength. The people of God had fasted and (we assume) prayed for her as she went to the king, endangering her own life for their sake. Her personal risk was emphasized in her words to Mordecai, "If I perish, I perish" (Esther 4:16). She would do her part, but she knew the outcome was in God's hands. She bowed not only to King Ahasuerus, but also to the Lord's sovereignty.

When Esther arrived at the throne room, she probably held her breath for the eternally long moment it took Ahasuerus to notice her and extend the golden scepter. You would have thought that, in a flood of relief, Esther would have blurted out her request immediately after the king asked, "What's the matter, Queen Esther?" but she waited. She did not act out of impatience but out of cultural protocol: "In the ancient Near East, one never made a major request right away, but paved the way with minor entreaties."[7]

At the banquet, the king knew there was something more important than food and wine on the mind of his beautiful queen. He asked again, "What is your request?" By now, I imagine she was bursting to state her true request, but she held it back one more time. Why the delay? Did she think the king needed a little more buttering up? Did she reason that a little more mystery would intrigue the king and sway him to her side? Did she simply lose her nerve?

Ultimately it was God who inspired Esther's delay. Esther might have desperately wanted to reveal her request. (Imagine serving two dinners to the creep who wants to destroy your people!) But God had a lot planned for the hours between the two banquets.

During that night, the king couldn't sleep and was reminded of how Mordecai saved his life. Haman built a gallows to destroy the defiant Jew, but he ended up having to honor him with a ticker-tape parade. While Esther slept, God rearranged events and rerouted the road Haman had so connivingly mapped out.

In periods of waiting, we feel helpless. Defenseless. Powerless. We want God to remove all the roadblocks to the itinerary we have chosen. But what if we perceived the barricades to our plans as our Father's invitation to sit back and watch Him work? What if we viewed the delays in our lives as God whispering, "Wait a little longer—watch and see what I will do. Trust Me"? With David, we can say, "O my Strength, I will *watch* for You, for You, O God, are my fortress" (Psalm 59:9).

What if we perceived the barricades to our plans as our Father's invitation to sit back and watch Him work?

When the bus of our lives has broken down and it seems we are stuck in a desolate desert of desperate circumstances, may we make the choice to trust. May we yield to God's sovereignty. May we, in the assurance of the Father's passionate love for us, confidently pray, "Thy will be done."

Courage in the Waiting

Esther needed endurance to wait through a year of beauty treatments. She needed tenacity to postpone her request to save her people. She needed God-given courage when she approached the king without being summoned.

It takes courage to wait.

David acknowledges this in Psalm 27:14:

> Wait for the Lord;
> be strong, and let your heart take courage;
> wait for the Lord!

In the seemingly strength-stripping deserts of waiting, we can become strong. We can collect confidence. I love how the ESV translates the Hebrew verb *chazaq* as "take courage." *Take* courage. We don't need to manufacture our own courage, our own determination, our own bravery. Through Word and Sacrament, the Holy Spirit will give us the strength to prevail as we wait. We receive courage as we remember that the God who has scheduled this stopping-over place is a loving, devoted, and faithful Father.

Do you feel like you are stuck in Death Valley? Perhaps you are in between praying for healing and receiving a cure. Maybe you see no hope of repentance from a wayward child. Or perhaps your desert is a drought of funds to pay the bills.

Esther's life teaches us that even in our desperate waiting places, we are not powerless. The Holy Spirit gives us the strength to wait well. To choose to use the waiting time to prepare for what's ahead. To rest in God's providence. To ask the Father for the next step. To grow in faith in the Lord's sovereignty.

In the bus ride of our lives, we can trust God to have a glorious destination planned. Even when Miracle White has broken down and we're stuck in a barren desert with the cockroaches, we know God's loving hand is directing every mile of our journey. Although it may seem to take forever to get the engine fixed, God's providence is working behind the scenes to get us back on the right road. And even when the ride still seems bumpy and meandering, we can trust that our journey will end in the heavenly home the Lord has prepared.

God's Grace in Esther's Story

Imagine Queen Esther approaching King Ahasuerus in his throne room, her knees knocking beneath her royal robes. Although she had done everything possible to gain a favorable response—fast, pray, put on her best clothes—she didn't know if the king would extend his golden scepter. She wasn't sure whether he would grant her mercy or sentence her to death.

One day we will also appear before a King—the King of kings. But because of our Lord's sacrifice on the cross, we do not need to wonder about His response. We don't have to worry if we have done enough. It is the Holy Spirit who gives us the gift of faith, washes us clean in the waters of Baptism, and dresses us in the robes of righteousness (Isaiah 61:10). When we have repented of our sins and received Christ's forgiveness and salvation, we can confidently approach His throne of grace and fully expect the King to extend His golden scepter of mercy.

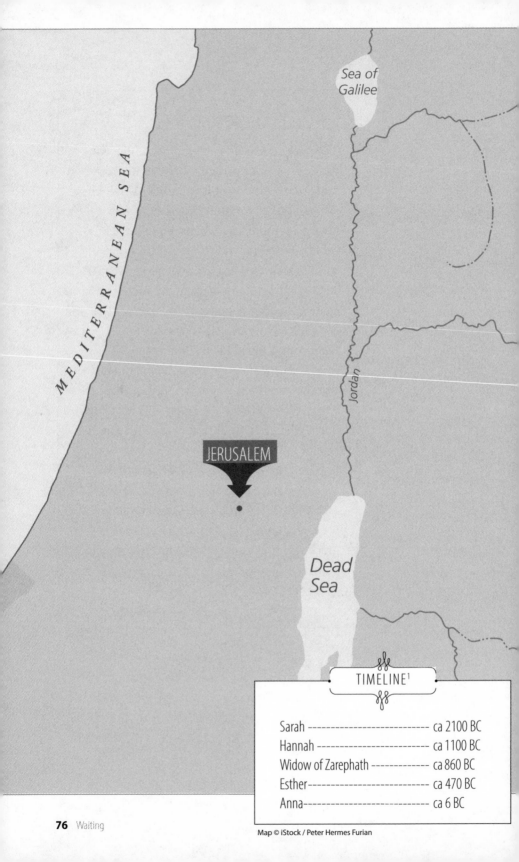

Sea of
Galilee

MEDITERRANEAN SEA

Jordan

JERUSALEM

Dead
Sea

TIMELINE[1]

Sarah	ca 2100 BC
Hannah	ca 1100 BC
Widow of Zarephath	ca 860 BC
Esther	ca 470 BC
Anna	ca 6 BC

Chapter 5

Anna

When Waiting Brings Purpose to Your Story

Luke 2:36–38

I love a good story. I like getting lost in a fictional world filled with interesting characters and an intriguing story line. Give me romance and mystery. Provide me with adventure and surprising plot twists.

However, in my own life, I greatly prefer a predictable narrative. I would like my life to have the pace of a well-crafted story of my own choosing. No unexpected plot twists for me, please. No long, drawn-out chapters of suspense. Just pleasant pages filled with laughter and friends. Years of successful work and close family ties. But why is that?

When my children grew up and I was facing an empty nest, the story line of my personal tale seemed to fizzle out. In my emptiness, I wondered if there were any meaningful chapters left. What was my purpose now?

Perhaps Anna felt the same way. This woman, whose short story is in the Gospel of Luke, probably wondered what her reason for living was after her husband died. Most likely she would have written her story differently if given the chance. She would have deleted the dramatic chapter entitled "Widowhood" and inserted pages and pages of happy family life. She would have edited out the loneliness and poverty and added chapters of purpose and prosperity.

If ever there was a life characterized by waiting, Anna's was it. She was born in a time when God's people prayed for political rescue and spiritual salvation. And while the nation of Israel collectively held its breath, Anna personally waited for God inside the walls of the temple. During decades of delay, she could not know that her seemingly unremarkable story would even be remembered.

Anna **77**

Setting the Scene

Anna lived during a time in history characterized as the climax of a very long wait for the people of Judea to be released from a long string of foreign rulers. In the previous four hundred years, they had been ruled by Cyrus the Great, Alexander the Great (and some of his generals), and now Herod the Great. And some of the rulers during those four centuries had been, well, not so great. Yes, Cyrus and Alexander had allowed the people of Israel to continue to worship the one true God. But the Seleucid rulers—descendants of one of Alexander's generals—opposed the Judean religion. The worst of the Seleucids, Antiochus IV, outlawed the observance of the Sabbath, the practice of circumcision, and the sacred temple sacrifices. He even desecrated the temple by erecting a statue of Zeus in the temple court and sacrificing a pig on the holy altar.

In 167 BC, some faithful Judeans, known as the Hasmonians, were able to defeat the Seleucids, and for fifteen years (until 142 BC), Judea was able to rule itself and worship the true God in peace. But then the Romans took over. And though Herod the Great, puppet of the Roman Empire, tried to appease the Judean people with many building projects, including the rebuilding of the Jerusalem temple, the Jews were tired of being under Caesar's thumb. They longed for freedom.

The Jews were also waiting for a prophet. It had been four hundred years since the prophet Malachi had written the last book of the Hebrew Scriptures (what we call the Old Testament). During this long "silent period," Jewish scholars worked on the Septuagint, a Greek translation of the Hebrew Scriptures. But the people of God were waiting for a fresh word from Him.

Most of all, the people were waiting for a Savior. For us, who live after the birth of Jesus, it's difficult to imagine the pain of this delay. Ever since the world was broken, its inhabitants were anticipating the Messiah. When Eve gave birth to her very first son, she declared, "I have gotten a man with the help of the LORD" (Genesis 4:1). In looking at the Hebrew phrasing, Luther and other theologians think that Eve was sure this son was the fulfillment of God's promise for a Savior. All the way through the Old Testament up to Malachi—who wrote, "The Lord whom you seek will suddenly come to His temple; and the messenger of the covenant in whom you delight, behold, He is coming" (Malachi 3:1)—the Jewish people were focused on their future salvation. When would this waiting end?

Anna's Story Begins

It is in this setting of waiting for a great deliverer of the Jews that the story of Anna takes place. This woman's story occupies only three verses in the Bible, but her character has a prominent role in the scene where Mary and Joseph bring the baby Jesus to the temple.

> And there was a prophetess, Anna the daughter of Phanuel, of the tribe of Asher. She was advanced in years, having lived with her husband seven years from when she was a virgin, and then as a widow until she was eighty-four. She did not depart from the temple, worshiping with fasting and prayer night and day. And coming up at that very hour she began to give thanks to God and to speak of Him to all who were waiting for the redemption of Jerusalem.
>
> Luke 2:36–38.

When Luke introduces us to Anna, he informs us that she was "advanced in years." She had been married and lived with her husband for seven years, but she had spent many more years as a widow. The Greek is unclear: either she was now eighty-four or she had been a widow for eighty-four years (making her about ninety-nine years old, assuming she married around the usual age of fifteen). Either way, Anna had experienced a long life and had lived most of it alone.

As a widow, Anna was probably destitute. We have already witnessed the desperate situation of the widow of Zarephath. The financial prospects for a widow had not improved much in the 850 years since then. Women could not easily obtain honorable employment, and there were no institutions set up to provide for those who had lost their husbands and their only means of support.

Luke also tells us that Anna "did not depart from the temple" (Luke 2:37). It is possible that as a poor widow, she had been given a room in the temple complex in return for some service.[2] There were modest apartments in the outer walls of the temple, thought to have been used by priests when they came for their two weeks of annual service.[3] Perhaps now in her advanced age, she no longer served in the temple formally, but she did not cease her service to God. Anna was truly devoted, "worshiping with fasting and prayer night and day." She continually worshiped the Lord, often ignoring her physical appetite and focusing on her hunger for God. She was a woman of prayer. We can imagine that as she heard the Hebrew Scriptures read, she constantly prayed for the fulfillment of God's promises and the coming of the Messiah.

Luke describes Anna as a prophetess. In the Bible, the term *prophet* denotes a spokesperson for God, a person "sent to speak the Lord's Word."[4] As a prophetess, Anna did not foretell the future, and it's doubtful that she ever got up on a soapbox to preach. But it may well be that as she spent her days in prayer in the temple complex, she encouraged other women with words of Scripture. She may have informally instructed those who gathered in the Court of Women.

Still, during those long years of prayer in the temple, Anna might have wondered why God had kept her on the earth for so long. What was her purpose? In a culture where a woman's primary roles were to help her husband and raise children, why was she still here? In the world's eyes, her usefulness was long spent. But in the last chapters of her life, the Lord pens a stunning plot twist.

It began on an ordinary day. Can you picture Anna? Perhaps she was making her way from her sparsely furnished apartment to the Court of Women. She wove her way through the crowds of worshipers already gathering. Her feet slowly shuffled along the stone courtyard. People around her craned their necks to admire the stunning structures. Voices marveling at the magnificence of the temple mingled with the bleating of sheep and the cooing of doves. And as she

WIDOWS IN NEW TESTAMENT TIMES

Widowhood was a common occurrence in Jesus' day, partly because men often married women ten to fifteen years younger in age. A widow in New Testament times not only experienced the loss of her life partner but often faced dire poverty. There were few respectable occupations for women, and the ancient world knew nothing about Social Security or life insurance.

The Early Church often stepped in to care for these women. In 1 Timothy 5, the apostle Paul encourages Timothy to keep a list of widows who need financial support. These women were to be at least sixty years old, faithful to their husbands, and known for their good works of hospitality and raising children. Widows on this list were those who had no one to care for them. Paul instructed everyone to care for the widows in their own families. Young widows were encouraged to remarry rather than rely on the church to support them and become idle gossips.

PROPHETESSES IN THE BIBLE

Luke tells us that Anna was a prophetess—one who spoke God's Word. There are several other women in the Bible who are described as prophetesses. Here are a few:

Miriam: The sister of Moses, she sang a song of victory after the Israelites fled Egypt, escaped Pharaoh's soldiers, and crossed the Red Sea (Exodus 15:20–21).

Deborah: Judges 4:4 tells us Deborah was a prophetess and a judge who settled disputes between people. She spoke God's word to Barak, calling him to lead the people in battle against the Canaanites.

Huldah: During King Josiah's reign, the priest Hilkiah discovered the Book of the Law in the temple. When the king heard God's Word, he commanded Hilkiah to inquire of the Lord. Hilkiah sought out Huldah the prophetess, who pronounced judgment on Judah for abandoning the Lord, but mercy for Josiah because of his repentant heart (2 Kings 22:8–20).

neared the court, the scent of incense intensified.

It was a new day, but somehow it seemed not much had changed. She had been here so many years. Day after day she observed the sacrificing of animals for her sin. Week after week she prayed for the Messiah to come. Year after year she waited and watched.

But as she entered the court, a small group of people caught her eye. An ordinary man and woman were with Simeon. Simeon, who had also waited and watched. Simeon, who once told her that the Holy Spirit had revealed that he would not die before he saw the Savior. There he was, near the Nicanor Gate, holding a baby, his eyes to heaven—and Anna could see joy in the tears streaming down his face. As she neared the little group, she heard Simeon's prayer:

"Lord, now You are letting Your
    servant depart in peace,
    according to Your word;
for my eyes have seen Your salvation
    that You have prepared in the
    presence of all peoples,
a light for revelation to the Gentiles,
and for glory to Your people Israel."
Luke 2:29–32

Anna's heart was in her throat. A day that began like any other had now become the moment she had hoped for all these years. A young couple who looked like they didn't have two shekels to rub together had arrived with the King of kings. The One who would change the world had arrived—in the form of a little baby.

Immediately Anna "began to give thanks to God and to speak of Him to all who were waiting for the redemption of Israel" (Luke 2:38). Her first response was of gratitude to the God who had fulfilled the longing of all their hearts. Perhaps, like Simeon, she spoke a beautiful poetic prayer.

But she didn't stop there. She shared the good news that had been revealed to her. Because she was present at the temple every day, she knew who the devoted worshipers were. She recognized those who, like her, were aching for the redemption of Israel. Can you see her approaching the faithful and whispering, "See that little baby over there? He's the one we've been waiting for!" or "Praise God with me today! God has fulfilled His promise. The Savior has come!"?

The climax of Anna's story had arrived.

PRESENTATION OF JESUS AT THE TEMPLE

Mary and Joseph had two purposes in going to the temple that day: the presentation of their firstborn and the purification of the mother. God's law required that every firstborn be dedicated to the Lord (Exodus 13:12–13). Animals were sacrificed, but firstborn children were redeemed—bought back—with an offering of five shekels (Numbers 18:15–16). Through this ritual, parents acknowledged that their child belonged to God. Mary and Joseph followed the law and brought Jesus to Jerusalem "to present Him to the Lord" (Luke 2:22).

Mary also needed to go to the temple for her purification. The flow of blood made a woman unclean and required a ritual sacrifice. Leviticus 12 instructs women to present a sacrifice forty days after the birth of a son. The sacrifice was to be a year-old lamb and a pigeon. But if the woman could not afford a lamb, she could bring two pigeons. Luke tells us that Mary and Joseph brought a pair of pigeons, informing us of their financial situation.

Purpose in the Pause in the Plotline

While Anna waited and worshiped in the temple all those decades, she may have wondered about her purpose in life. I, too, experienced a waiting time—questioning my purpose. Back in chapter 1, I told you about praying for a child. I was so thankful when, after we had endured a couple of years of waiting, God granted my request for children and blessed us with a daughter.

We then hoped and prayed through another miscarriage and more delay until our son was born. But we felt blessed—and busy. Life was crammed full of activity. Diapers and 2 a.m. feedings. Preschool and playdates. Homeschooling and tennis meets. Of course, there were days when I waited and wished for more time for myself, but I loved (almost) every minute of the parenting years.

So when homeschooling was finished, when my younger child graduated from high school, when the older got married and moved to Texas, my home and my life seemed rather empty.

Not that my kids didn't love me or that my husband had abandoned me, but I wondered, *If your kids don't need daily mothering, what is a mother to do? What am I supposed to do with my life?*

In the years leading up to my son's high school graduation, I had seen the writing on the walls of our homeschool and knew I would soon need to find something else to fill the hours usually spent making lesson plans, teaching, and correcting tests. So when I was asked to be a speaker for an interdenominational organization, I tentatively said yes. *Is this what God wants me to do with my life?*

But the speaking engagements were few and far between and there were still many hours to fill. My son was living at home but spent most of his time at college classes and campus hangouts. My daughter called from Texas for long chats, but it wasn't the same as going out to lunch at our favorite Italian restaurant and eating our body weight in breadsticks. So instead of lunch dates, I filled my time with pity parties.

Something had to change. After a couple more months of feeling-sorry-for-myself soirees, I remembered that before I took on the monumental task of homeschooling, I had loved to write. So to take my mind off the emptiness in my heart, I started to fill pages with words. *Maybe writing a book is my new purpose?*

"Maybe" was right. I soon became more discouraged and confused than ever. Anyone who has ventured into the world of writing knows that it comes with its own waiting rooms. After I had written a proposal for a book idea, I sent it out to agents and publishers—and waited. Responses were slow in coming, and when they did come, they were all of the this-book-does-not-meet-our-publishing-needs-at-this-time variety. Maybe writing a book was *not* my new purpose.

Waiting for Purpose

Have you experienced a pause in the story you envisioned for your life too? Maybe, like Anna, you have lost a loved one. Or like me, you are facing an empty nest. Perhaps you've moved across the country for your husband's work, but you're missing the ministry you were involved with in your former city. Or you're now a stay-at-home mom, and changing diapers just doesn't seem as important as the influential corporate work you used to do.

Thankfully, Anna's story in Scripture gives us some answers when we ask, what's my purpose now?

God can use a time of waiting to help us find purpose right where we are. Perhaps after her husband died, Anna felt that the climax of her life had come and gone. Her husband was no longer with her, and if she had ever had children, it was likely they had also passed away. (If they were still living, she probably would have lived with them.) In a culture where a woman's primary duties were caring for a family, what was her purpose in life?

But a break in the typical plotline for women brought Anna a new purpose. She now spent her days in the temple, worshiping and praying. She was known as a speaker of God's Word. As a young woman, Anna probably never envisioned this as her role, but it's clear that she was now devoted to it.

Anna's life demonstrates that we can all have purpose right where we are. When our dreams have died and our reason for living is pulled out from under our feet, God can give us new direction. He can use our talents, our gifts, and even our disappointments in ways we never could have imagined.

After my kids grew up, I floundered for a new purpose. I had dedicated

DEVOTED TO GOD'S SERVICE

Martin Luther wrote, "We love God above all things when we cling to Him alone as our God and gladly devote our lives to His service".[5] Anna devoted her life to God's service, worshiping the Lord day and night in His temple. While we cannot spend all our time in the Lord's house, we can still live our lives dedicated to God. Spend some time thinking of how this looks in your life. How do you already live committed to God's service? What habits, routines, or attitudes might you change to make this more of a reality?

my days to my children, educating and caring for them. Once that role was finished, I felt left without direction. I remember talking with frazzled-looking young mothers and telling them that I didn't covet their sleepless nights, but I still envied them. As a mother, I always felt I had a clear purpose—a noble task of raising children.

> What if we use our waiting time to ask, "God, what do You want me to do right now? right here?"

In a way, I felt that the climax of my life had come and gone. Intellectually, I realized that I needed to stop looking back. Deep inside, I knew I needed to grab on to God's words, "I have . . . plans for welfare and not for evil, to give you a future and a hope" (Jeremiah 29:11). But I struggled with this.

It took two years of prayer before God eventually led me to a role of communicating His Word. Finally, one day, my husband and I came home from a vacation and discovered this message on our answering machine: "It's our pleasure to share some good news—we want to publish your book! I know we said no before, but we've changed our minds. Call us back, and we'll talk details."

That phone call started my journey of publishing Bible studies. Writing and speaking have become a new purpose in my life. For the present time, God has placed a calling on my life to share His transforming grace with women around the country. Like Anna, I get to point people to Immanuel— God with us. All that waiting led me to a brand-new challenge. As a homeschool mom, I never would have imagined that I would someday spend my time writing and speaking.

What if in our waiting, we quit wishing for our past purposes? And what if we reject the idea that we can only do important things when our life is picture-perfect?

What if we use our waiting time to ask, "God, what do You want me to do right now? right here?"

God can use a waiting season to change our expectations. It may take a time of delay to find the new purpose God has for you. It may take a protracted pause in your own plans to be open to God's design for your life. Especially if you're stubborn like me. During my two years of asking, "What now, Lord?" I tried many different solutions. I attempted to expand my piano teaching business. But my efforts failed again and again. I tried several different volunteer opportunities. Yet nothing seemed to be the right fit. Eventually, waiting erased my self-sufficiency and my demands to be the author of my own life story. And it was then that I became open to the story that God wanted to write for my life.

Anna is an excellent example of someone who waited without expectations. During her lifetime, many people were looking for a Messiah. Just look at the crowds of people who gathered to see John the Baptist and his message of a coming Savior. But most people were anticipating a powerful political leader. They were waiting for a hero who would conquer the Romans and free them from oppression.

That day in the temple, only two people recognized the child of a peasant couple as the Messiah. There was no trumpet fanfare announcing His arrival. No formal proclamation that the King had come. God revealed His Son's appearance to one lowly gentleman and an elderly woman. The majority of the Judeans missed it because of their preconceived expectations.

We're often like those Judeans. We think, *My purpose needs to look like an exciting career or a perfect family. I need to have a powerful influence or my life won't count.* But what if your purpose is like Anna's—to faithfully worship and pray every day? To show up and worship year after year? To encourage those around you who need the Good News of a Savior?

I'm beginning to pray, "Lord, forgive me when I expect You to work according to my plan. When I forget that You are 'able to do far more abundantly than all that we ask or think' (Ephesians 3:20). Thank You for Your forgiveness and grace. Help me not to wait for an assignment that is deemed important by the world. Open my eyes to the work You have prepared for me, big or small."

Perhaps those who realize that God-given purpose comes in all shapes and sizes are the ones who find it. Maybe those who wait without preconceived expectations are the ones who notice God's action in their lives.

God can use a waiting time to help us find our true worth. Not only am I tempted to dismiss any life purpose that doesn't look exciting or influential, I often base my self-worth on my ability—or inability—to accomplish something "significant." If I achieve an important goal or get a little applause, I feel valuable. But if my work is rejected or someone else gets the attention I crave, I deem myself worthless.

One thing I love about Anna's story is that God did not reveal His Son to the richest or most successful woman. He didn't unveil the significance of the baby Jesus to the loveliest or youngest. God chose to reveal the fact that the

Messiah had come in the form of an infant to a poor, elderly woman.

In fact, God gave this senior citizen the mission of telling the Good News of Jesus to "all who were waiting for the redemption of Jerusalem" (Luke 2:38). I can't imagine an earthly king giving an eighty-plus-year-old woman the important assignment of announcing his son's birth. Can you? But that is exactly what the Father did. God gives important roles in His kingdom to everyone. We see in Anna's story that He often chooses the poor and marginalized. Those without husbands or children. Those without worldly honor or influence. In Anna's story, we see that achieving great purpose in life is not reserved for the young and beautiful or the successful and significant.

> Your worth is not based on success or failure. Your value is solely in your status as the daughter of the Most High King.

When I was waiting for purpose, I felt like one big failure. Every book manuscript I sent out was returned with a big (but polite) "No thank you." I wasn't accomplishing anything (except for banging my head against a myriad of publishing house doors). But in the waiting, I began to sense God whispering, "Heavenly status is not measured by the number of books sold or the size of your audience. Your worth is not based on success or failure. Your value is solely in your status as the daughter of the Most High King."

Waiting Patiently— Yeah, Right

During my period of waiting for a new purpose, I began studying the word *wait* in Scripture. I got out my hefty concordance and began reading every verse in the Bible that contained that word. One of the passages that I turned to again and again was Psalm 40:1–3:

> I waited patiently for the LORD;
> He inclined to me and heard my cry.
> He drew me up from the pit of

SHARING THE GOOD NEWS

Anna wasted no time in revealing the good news that the Messiah had come. She immediately began sharing the news flash with all her fellow worshipers who were awaiting a Savior. Who in your life needs to hear the Good News of Jesus? Spend some time in prayer today for them, asking that God would give you the best opportunity and the right words to speak. Pray that the Spirit would open their ears and hearts to hear.

> destruction,
>   out of the miry bog,
> and set my feet upon a rock,
>   making my steps secure.
> He put a new song in my mouth,
>   a song of praise to our God.
> Many will see and fear,
>   and put their trust in the LORD.

"Waiting patiently for the LORD"—yeah, right. No one who knew me well would have described me in those terms. But I wanted to learn. What could King David's words teach me about waiting well?

When I read that the Lord "inclined to me and heard my cry" (Psalm 40:1), I could picture God leaning in, listening to my sobbing, hearing my shouts for answers. Even though I hadn't received a tangible reply yet, God's Word reminded me that He was paying attention.

God "drew me up from the pit of destruction" (Psalm 40:2). I wasn't actually in a pit of destruction. But I had dug my own pit of despair with a shovel of incessant griping and complaining. God assured me that if I let Him, He could pull me out of that ditch of dejection.

"He put a new song in my mouth, a song of praise to our God" (Psalm 40:3). Perhaps a key to waiting well is glorifying God instead of whining. I definitely didn't feel that I could do this on my own, but God promised to put a song of praise in my mouth.

When I read the last part of verse 3, my waiting story began to make more sense: "Many will see and fear, and put their trust in the LORD." Maybe the longer the wait, the more people would see God's power at work. Perhaps when a publisher finally said yes, it would be all the more evident that it was God's doing and more people would be drawn to trust in Him.

A Better Story Needs a Little Suspense

Maybe you are experiencing your own wait for purpose. Maybe, like me, you feel the debilitating effects of an empty nest and you ask, "What does a mother do when she can't mother anymore?" Maybe you are just starting out in life and you have no earthly idea how to respond to the constant questions of "What are your goals?" Perhaps you're in midlife and you're *still* wondering, "What will I do when I grow up?" Or maybe you're advanced in years like

Anna, and you're questioning if your life has any purpose at all anymore.

Let me tell you: Every moment of waiting that God places in your life matters.

Have you noticed that your favorite novels have the necessary element of suspense? that you like the book a little less when you can guess how the story ends from the very first chapter? God is writing an excellent story for your life, and suspense is a necessary element. It's during those waiting periods that God develops our patience, molds our character, and teaches us our most crucial life lessons.

I love to read. And in my favorite stories, the hardships the heroine experiences make her stronger or smarter. The obstacles in her way guide her to deeper relationships. Overcoming problems leads to unexpected rewards. At the end of the book, you discover each plot twist had a purpose. Every ordeal finally makes sense.

The novels I like the least are the ones where the ending feels . . . unfinished. The protagonist strives to rise above her problems. She works to surmount the barriers in her way. And she almost succeeds. But in the end, nothing is resolved. After chapters and chapters of searching for the love of her life, the heroine of the story never finds him. Or the lawyer works to overcome big bad corporations but loses his law practice, and the battle must continue without him. Nothing makes sense.

While some literature may favor the more "realistic" ending, those plot conclusions make me want to throw the book at the wall. Reading a dissatisfying story seems like one big waste of time.

And maybe that is one reason we hate waiting. We're afraid the prolonged time spent in a suspenseful chapter of our lives will culminate in one big disappointment.

That's when we need to remember that God is the author of our stories.

Even though we can't see how all the twists and turns in our plotline are going to work out, *He can*. Because God is at work in our lives, all of our hardships can strengthen our faith in Him. The obstacles in our lives can drive us to a deeper relationship with our loving Father. As the Spirit helps us overcome problems, we see the rewards of peace and contentment.

> Every moment of waiting that God places in your life matters.

> We're afraid the prolonged time spent in a suspenseful chapter of our lives will culminate in one big disappointment.

Waiting well means trusting that God is at work even in long chapters of uncertainty or heartache. We see from Anna's story that the Lord can give purpose to our lives even in the middle of delay. That God-given purpose comes in all shapes and sizes, and it is not granted solely to those with prominent positions or hefty bank accounts. We wait well when we are like Anna, who was waiting for the Christ, because it is only through the Messiah that any of us can have a happy ending to our story.

If Anna had been the sole author of her tale, she probably would have edited out any references to death and loneliness and inserted happy chapters of family life. But God was the creator of her life narrative. And in the closing chapters, she could see how the story made sense. Her waiting story was the epilogue to the centuries of waiting for the promised Messiah. She was one of the first people to recognize that Christ had come!

So while you might wish to write a more predictable story for your life, be confident that in every plot twist, God has a purpose. Every agonizing difficulty can be transformed in God's hand.

And while you're still in this confusing middle-of-the-story time, remember: God is leaning in. He sees you as you wait. He hears your cries. He reassures you that He has the ending of your tale all worked out. Every suspenseful plot element has purpose in your magnificent story.

God's Grace in Anna's Story

When Luke introduces us to Anna, he tells us that she was the "daughter of Phanuel, of the tribe of Asher" (Luke 2:36). When we look back at the history of Israel, we see that it is remarkable that a member of that tribe is present at the temple at all.

Asher was one of the northern tribes that rebelled against the Lord and worshiped false gods. It was part of the nation that was conquered by the Assyrians and carried off into captivity. Very few of these captives ever returned to Israel. So how did a descendant of a rebellious, unbelieving, and exiled tribe end up as a devoted worshiper of Yahweh?

Only by God's grace.

Maybe you come from a questionable past. Or from a long line of rebels and doubters. It doesn't matter. In His grace, God loves us all. The Lord invites all nobodies, nonconformists, cynics, and skeptics to a personal relationship with Him. Through the redeeming work of His Son, we can all be washed clean and come into His presence.

— • — • — • — • — • -

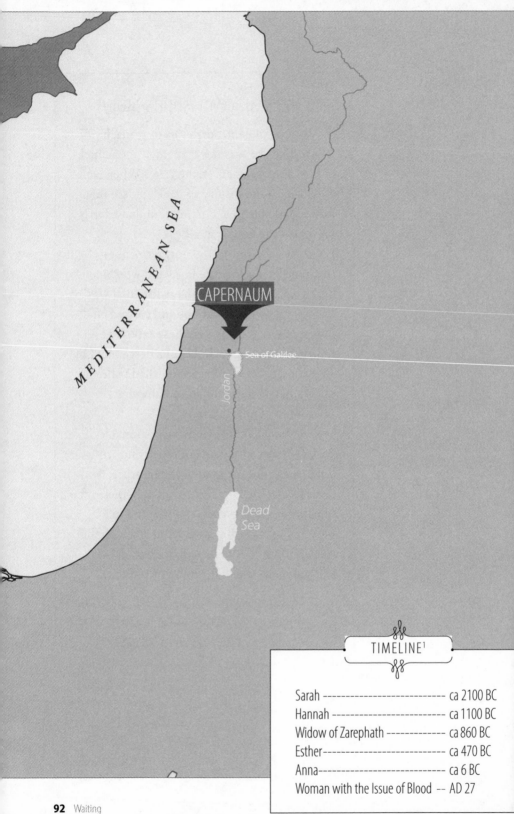

CAPERNAUM

MEDITERRANEAN SEA

Sea of Galilee

Jordan

Dead Sea

TIMELINE[1]

Sarah	ca 2100 BC
Hannah	ca 1100 BC
Widow of Zarephath	ca 860 BC
Esther	ca 470 BC
Anna	ca 6 BC
Woman with the Issue of Blood	AD 27

Chapter 6

The Woman with the Issue of Blood
When Waiting Draws You to Jesus

Matthew 9:20–22; Mark 5:25–34; Luke 8:43–48

> Soothing music wafts through the space. Matching chairs
> beautify the area. Artful centerpieces sit on tables, and
> peaceful landscape paintings grace the walls.

If it wasn't for the faint smell of antiseptic that permeates the air and the silence of the worried people that fills the room, it might be a pleasant place to relax.

But no matter how beautiful a doctor's waiting room is, waiting can be an agonizing experience. If you're sick, you simply want to see the physician, get your medication, and get back home to bed. If you're waiting with someone you love who is ill, you're concerned for his or her health. And if you're not sure what's wrong, it feels like worry and anxiety are sitting on the chairs on either side of you, whispering worst-case scenarios in your ears.

Unfortunately, my mother has been in many beautiful rooms filled with worry and anxiety, waiting for her name to be called. Waiting for her turn to see the doctor. Waiting for an answer to her pain. Mom's agony has sent her to dozens of doctors and medical practitioners. And yet, she has found little relief.

She can relate well to the woman in the New Testament who experienced a twelve-year waiting period for healing. This biblical woman's waiting room became a type of prison. Although she searched for answers, for healing, for relief, she found none—until she met Jesus.

Setting the Scene

A crowd was gathering. Perhaps a fisherman mending his nets on the shore of the Sea of Galilee had spotted Jesus and His disciples in the boat nearing Capernaum. Maybe it was a boy skipping stones on the lake who first saw the Teacher approaching. Someone mentioned Jesus was back in town, and it didn't take long for word to spread. Before Jesus' boat even reached the shore, people had gathered. I imagine some wanted to see for themselves this man from Nazareth that they had heard so much about. Some wanted to hear Him speak again. And some longed for healing.

Jesus' reputation as a healer had already been established. He had helped people with unclean spirits and leprosy. He had restored sight and speech. In the synagogue, He had healed a withered hand. All over Galilee, crowds thronged to see Jesus, and people with diseases pressed in to touch Him (Mark 3:10).

CAPERNAUM

Capernaum was a sizable town in Jesus' day. Located on the northwestern shore of the Sea of Galilee, its residents made their living from agriculture, fishing, and trade.

Several of the twelve disciples were from Capernaum. Jesus met Matthew when he was sitting at the tax collector's booth near the lake. Four fishermen from the town— James, John, Andrew, and Peter—all left their nets at the Sea of Galilee and followed Jesus when He called them. Peter's home became a base for Jesus' ministry in the region.

Jesus healed many citizens of Capernaum from diseases and demon possession. One notable person He healed was Peter's mother-in-law (Mark 1:29–31).

One Woman

There was one woman in Capernaum whose heart must have danced when she heard Jesus was back in town. She was desperate for healing. For twelve long years, she had suffered from an issue of blood. This was so much more than the menstrual cycle of other women. It seemed to never stop.[2] The relentless blood flow drained her finances. The Gospel of Mark tells us she had "suffered much under many physicians, and had spent all that she had, and was no better but rather grew worse" (Mark 5:26). It had sapped her strength. Most likely she felt weak and anemic from the constant loss of blood. Even her relationships were affected. Levitical law declared her unclean. This meant sexual relations with a husband would make him unclean too. Anyone who touched her bed, her chair, her person became ritually impure. The disease had turned her into a pariah. She yearned for a cure.

How did she know that Jesus was coming? Was she near her window when children in the street shouted to one another that the Teacher was on His way? Did she overhear a neighbor tell a friend that the Healer was back in town? I wonder if she had to give herself a pep talk. To tell herself that this was her last chance for health. To force her body out of bed, even if she was feeling especially dizzy that day.

Perhaps her heart sank when she went out into the street. So many people—how could she ever reach Jesus? And Jairus, the ruler of the synagogue, was already telling Jesus about his sick daughter, imploring the Healer to come to his house. Of *course* Jesus would go to the home of an important official. She, on the other hand, had no chance. She was less than a nobody. Would Jesus even listen?

Still, she might have told herself, *I don't need to bother Him. I don't need to slow Him down. I only need to touch the tassel of His robe, and I know He will make me well.*

So she shuffled through the crowd—perhaps keeping her veil low so people wouldn't recognize her, and hugging her arms tight to her body to avoid touching anyone—edging

LEVITICAL LAW ON BLEEDING

The woman who suffered twelve long years with bleeding was considered unclean according to Jewish law.

Leviticus 15 gives the details of ritual uncleanness from bleeding. If a woman was menstruating, she was impure for seven days. And whoever touched her during those seven days became unclean until evening. Everything she sat on or lay on would also be ritually impure, contaminating anyone who touched them. If a man had sexual intercourse with a menstruating woman, he was also made unclean for seven days.

But if a woman had a discharge of blood for many days—not her monthly period—she would be unclean for all the days of the bleeding, plus seven days after the bleeding stopped. Again, anyone who touched her, her bed, or her chair would become unclean until evening.

The menstruating woman automatically became clean after the seven days. But the woman with the extended bleeding would have to go to the tabernacle or temple on the eighth day after the bleeding stopped. There she would sacrifice two turtledoves or pigeons as an offering to the Lord, and she would be purified.

closer and closer to Jesus. People were pressing in on all sides. But finally she was within arm's reach of Jesus. She could see the blue fringe of His robe hanging down His back. *There!* She reached out and touched it.

Instantly, she was well. She felt whole. The flow of blood had stopped. Perhaps she felt like shouting "Hallelujah!" but didn't want to draw attention to herself. She probably tried to back out of the crowd as it continued to push forward toward Jairus's home.

But suddenly Jesus stopped and turned around. "Who touched My clothes?" He asked. The disciples almost laughed and said, "You see the crowd is pressing around You, and yet You say, 'Who touched Me?'" (Mark 5:31).

It seemed a foolish question. Certainly most of the people nearby had bumped into Him as they were walking down the street. Perhaps those closest to Him now backed away, puzzled. Did they look at one another, wondering if they had done something wrong?

Jesus continued to look around. He said, "Someone

UNCLEAN AND CLEAN

What did it mean to be unclean?

According to Leviticus 11–15, there were several ways to become unclean, including skin diseases, childbirth, touching something dead, and eating unclean foods.

Unclean persons could not go to the tabernacle or temple because they would defile the holy space. An unclean priest could not perform his sacred duties. And if a layperson became impure, he could not eat consecrated food (Leviticus 7:20–21) and would have to celebrate Passover a month late (Numbers 9:6–13).

The way to become clean again varied with the severity of impurity. The most severe uncleanness—skin disease—involved a seven-day ritual including having a priest confirm the healing, sacrificing birds, shaving all hair from the head, bathing, and washing clothes in water (Leviticus 14:1–32). On the other end of severity, a person becoming impure through contact with an unclean person merely had to take a ritual bath and wait until evening to become clean (Leviticus 15:21).

The main rationale of the purity laws was to emphasize that God is holy and man is contaminated. Although uncleanness was not usually caused by sin, there is an analogy between uncleanness and sin. We, as sinful human beings, must be purified in order to approach a holy God.[3]

touched Me, for I perceive that power has gone out from Me" (Luke 8:46).

The woman realized Jesus was not going to give up. Trembling, she fell at His feet. "Lord, I am the one who touched You." Did she fear a reprimand? Mark says she "told Him the whole truth" (Mark 5:33). Was she afraid the Healer would berate her for making Him unclean?

Fear and shame were unwarranted. Jesus spoke gently to her: "Daughter, your faith has healed you. Go in peace and be freed from your suffering."

Just then, someone from Jairus's house came and told him, "Your daughter is dead. Why trouble the Teacher anymore?" At these words, Jesus turned from the woman, tried to reassure Jairus, and continued on to the synagogue ruler's house with Peter, James, and John. The rest of the crowd dispersed.

Can you imagine the woman's joy? She was healed. She was whole. She had seen Jesus and heard Him call her "Daughter." I can picture her running home—because now she could.

Twelve Years of Waiting

Twelve years is a long time to be sick. Twelve years of bleeding. Twelve years of medical bills. Twelve years of watching others shrink from her touch. Twelve years of isolation from the worship community.

This woman who endured years of suffering doesn't even get her name mentioned in the biblical account. The Early Church thought she deserved a name, so they called her Veronica.[4] This may or may not have been her real name, but so we don't have to keep calling her "the bleeding woman," I will use the name Veronica.

Veronica is an inspiration to all of us who have been stuck in a waiting room of life. She demonstrates what to do when we are faced with delay: go to Jesus.

How did she know to draw near to Jesus? She had likely heard the stories of His miraculous healing power. In her own town of Capernaum, four men had brought their paralyzed friend to an overcrowded event, cut a hole in the roof, and lowered him down—right in front of Jesus. And when the Teacher had told the man who couldn't walk, "Pick up your bed and go home," he *did*! On another occasion, the Roman centurion in town had asked Jesus to heal his servant. "No need to come to my house," the centurion had said. "Just speak the word and he will be healed." And he was!

Drawing Near to Jesus

Veronica was sure Jesus was the answer to her problem—so she went to Him. Whether we have been waiting for twelve days, twelve months, or twelve years, drawing close to Jesus is the best thing we can do. Jesus welcomes us all when we are in one of life's waiting rooms. He invites us to come to Him in prayer for help and for peace. He beckons us to come to His Holy Meal in faith and in confidence that we will be healed of our sin-sickness.

Jesus invites us to come to Him for help. Our loving Savior longs for us to come to Him. And yet we often try every other option first.

For twelve years, Veronica went to doctor after doctor. She spent all her money and wasn't any better. In fact, she was worse. The Talmud (a compilation of the oral teachings of many rabbis) lists eleven different cures for bleeding problems like hers.[5] Maybe Veronica tried them all. Perhaps she paid dearly for Persian onions boiled in cumin or safflower boiled in wine.[6] Maybe a renowned healer led her to a place where two roads met, gave her a cup of wine to hold, and then had someone come from behind and shout, "Arise from thy flux!" Or perhaps she was desperate enough to try the cure that involved digging seven ditches, burning cuttings of vines in the ditches, then sitting in the ashes of each hole with a cup of wine while someone said, "Arise from thy flux."[7] Hmm . . . I wonder why she wasn't healed?

It's no surprise that after such "cures," Veronica was drawn to Jesus. Nothing else had worked.

I have to admit that I, too, am more drawn to Jesus when I am waiting. When things are going smoothly and my plans are progressing, I sometimes forget my critical need for a Savior. But when life comes to a standstill and I've tried everything I can think of—except maybe for standing in an intersection with a glass of wine—I cry out to Jesus. Through God's Word, the Holy Spirit reminds me, "Draw near to God, and He will draw near to you" (James 4:8). God is near in His Word, in the Divine Service, in the body and blood of our Savior.

Jesus invites us to come to Him with confidence. Truthfully, I used to think it was rather unkind of Jesus to call Veronica out of her anonymity. It seems to me that she wanted attention about as much as a diva wants obscurity.

I can't imagine the isolation and shame she experienced. Anyone who came into physical contact with her became "unclean until the evening"

NO LONGER UNTOUCHABLE

Imagine twelve years of no hugs or kisses from friends and family. Twelve years of no intimacy between spouses. Maybe Veronica had a few close friends who risked temporary uncleanness to comfort and care for her. Maybe she had a self-sacrificing husband who loved her through the twelve years without physical intimacy. But it's more likely that people avoided her and took a step away if she came too near. It is probable that she never married or that if she was married, her husband issued her a certificate of divorce when he grew tired of a woman who couldn't fulfill her wifely duties.

Jesus changed all of that with His healing power. Perhaps one of the reasons He drew attention to this woman who had suffered so long was to let everyone know she was no longer "untouchable."

(Leviticus 15:19). She would have been as untouchable as a leper.

Her enforced isolation would have made attention from a crowd of people more than a little uncomfortable. Because of her sickness, there was a risk that those present would cry in horror at the thought of having touched her in the crush of the crowd. When she came forward in response to Jesus' question "Who touched Me?" she came in fear and trembling.

She approached in fear of being reprimanded for touching the great Teacher and in fear of being made a public spectacle. Although she had taken care to touch only the very tip of His garment, she knew she had risked making Him unclean. Would Jesus be angry with her?

But the first thing Jesus said to her was "Daughter." A gentle term. A tender designation. He wanted the woman to know that He wasn't annoyed with her. He didn't want her to feel guilt over "stealing" a blessing. Her touch of faith was not only the beginning of physical healing; it was the start of a personal relationship.

Jesus was a busy man that day in Capernaum. Throngs of people followed Him as He was on His way to heal the dying daughter of a prominent man. Yet He stopped to talk with Veronica. He didn't need to stop to heal her. Her condition had already been cured. He didn't need to stop to find out who touched His robe. As omniscient God, He already knew.

And yet He stopped. Jesus paused on His way to a very important daughter to give His undivided attention to another daughter who was more lowly—in the eyes of the crowd. One who was unclean. Insignificant. The Savior of the world searched the throng, inviting her to come to Him.

Jesus pauses to give each of us His undivided attention. I don't have to be a well-known community leader. I don't need to be a *New York Times* best-selling author or the blogger who garners a million visits per month. It doesn't matter that I'm not the CEO of a Fortune 500 company or even the mom who has it all together. I don't even have to be a "good" Christian. Jesus searches the crowd for me, for each one of us, beckoning us to come to Him. He invites us to come in confidence of His love and grace.

Jesus invites us to come to Him in faith. After Jesus tenderly addressed the

DRAW NEAR WITH CONFIDENCE

Hebrews 4:16 tells us, "Let us then with confidence draw near to the throne of grace, that we may receive mercy and find grace to help in time of need." The Holy Spirit gives us confidence and strength to reach out to Jesus even in our sinful, unclean state. Christ's grace immediately cleanses our souls.

woman as "Daughter," He commended her for her faith: "Your faith has made you well." The woman's certainty of Jesus' ability to heal was what drew her to Him in the first place. She might have kept repeating to herself, *If I just touch His clothes, just the edge of His clothes, I'll be well.* Perhaps her faith was immature and maybe even a little superstitious, but Jesus praised her for it. He wanted her to know it wasn't a "magic" tassel on a robe that had cured her. It was faith that appropriated the gift of healing. "Her faith was the means whereby healing was received from the outpouring of Jesus' power and grace."[8]

Jesus valued faith. He praised a Roman centurion and a Canaanite woman for their great faith. He shook His head over those who exhibited doubt and distrust. At least four times, Jesus rebuked the disciples for their "little faith" (Matthew 8:26; 14:31; 16:8; 17:20). In Jesus' own hometown of Nazareth, He didn't perform mighty miracles because its residents exhibited a lack of faith (Mark 6:1–6).

God's gifts are received by faith. He doesn't force them on anyone. We need a receptive attitude. Faith—itself a gift—is the open hand that accepts the blessings of God.

Many other people bumped into Jesus that day in Capernaum. The disciples told Jesus, "Master, the crowds surround You and are pressing in on You!" (Luke 8:45). But not all of them were healed. Not all of them received what they were waiting for. Not all of them drew on the power of God.

A STORY INTERRUPTED

The story of Veronica is an interruption in the account of Jairus's daughter. On the surface, it may appear the two women didn't have much in common. One was only a girl, the other a grown woman. One was the daughter of a prominent citizen; the other was considered a nobody.

But if we look more closely, we see elements that tie the two stories together. The number *12* is significant to both. Jairus's daughter was twelve years old. Veronica had been ill for twelve years. Both were healed through contact with Jesus. The Healer took Jairus's daughter's hand and said, "Child, arise" (Luke 8:54). Veronica touched Jesus' clothes. Faith was crucial in both cases. Jesus encouraged Jairus with these words: "Do not fear; only believe, and she will be well" (Luke 8:50), and He praised the bleeding woman's faith.

The two stories intertwine. Together they remind us that whatever the status we have in this world, we need Jesus. And no matter who we are, Jesus is more than willing to stop and help.

Only the woman who believed in Christ's ability to heal was cured. Only the woman who reached out in faith caused Jesus to perceive power going out from Him.

Perhaps the other people in the crowd came out of curiosity or to hear a captivating sermon. They didn't come to be transformed. Casual contact with Jesus won't alter our lives. But coming to Jesus with an expectation that He will renew us and make us whole changes everything.

Do I expect something wonderful when I meet with Jesus? Do I approach Him in faith, ready to receive His gifts? Or do I think it's enough to cross His path? Make casual contact. Go to church. Check off quiet time on my to-do list. Do I bump into Him but without faith? without consciously receiving His power and grace?

When Jesus stopped in the middle of the trip to Jairus's house, He gave Veronica an opportunity to profess her faith. She came to Him in a trembling ball of tears, but she "declared in the presence of all the people why she had touched Him, and how she had been immediately healed" (Luke 8:47).

What I saw as an uncomfortable assault on her privacy, Jesus meant as a faith-building exercise.

> But coming to Jesus with an expectation that He will renew us and make us whole changes everything.

Romans 10:10 states, "For with the heart one believes and is justified, and with the mouth one confesses and is saved." There is an important connection between faith expressed outwardly and possessed inwardly. Declaring faith gives evidence of an active trust, and it witnesses to others.

When I am in one of life's waiting rooms, I can grumble, complain, and constantly check my watch. Or I can use the delay as an opportunity to declare my faith. Waiting well means drawing near to Jesus when my life is a mess. It means coming to the God who is able to heal all my pain and heartaches—even if He may not do so before heaven. It means repenting of my doubts and receiving Christ's forgiveness. It means pouring out my discouragement and frustration and receiving His healing gifts of His presence and love. I wait well when I pray the prayer of King Jehoshaphat: "We do not know what to do, but our eyes are on You" (2 Chronicles 20:12).

THE FRINGE OF HIS GARMENT

In Luke's account of the bleeding woman, he writes, "She came up behind Him and touched the fringe of His garment" (Luke 8:44). Although you might be picturing some retro 1960s fashion fad, the Greek word used here—*kraspedon*—tells us that the "fringe" was a tassel that Jews attached to their cloaks to remind them of God's Law.[9]

In Numbers 15, God told Moses to instruct the people to sew tassels with a blue cord on the corners of their garments. The Lord said, "It shall be a tassel for you to look at and remember all the commandments of the LORD, to do them, not to follow after your own heart and your own eyes" (Numbers 15:39).

Although we often picture the woman kneeling on the ground to touch the hem of Jesus' clothes, this is unlikely. Because of the crowd, she would have been trampled. Instead, it is more likely that Jesus had one corner of His cloak thrown over His shoulder and the woman was able to touch the tassel hanging down His back.

Jesus invites us to come to Him—for peace. Veronica came to Jesus for healing. And received it. She knew the instant she touched that blue tassel that the bleeding had stopped and her body was made whole. But when Jesus spoke to her, He not only assured her of physical healing; He also gave her a blessing of peace. He said, "Daughter, your faith has made you well; go in peace, and be healed of your disease" (Mark 5:34).

The Greek word translated as "peace" is *eirene*, the same word used in

Romans 5:1: "Therefore, since we have been justified by faith, we have peace with God through our Lord Jesus Christ." This kind of peace is the condition of no longer being at war with God—no longer separated from His love.

> Our Savior grants the tranquility that comes with knowing that He is sitting right beside us, holding our hands in the waiting rooms of life.

Veronica could not have this kind of peace until she had been "made well." The words "made well" are from the Greek word *sozo*, which means "to save, keep safe and sound, to rescue from danger or destruction."[10] In the New Testament, *sozo* was used not only in the sense of saving from sickness or danger but also saving from sin. It is the same word used for "save" in Matthew 1:21: "She will bear a son, and you shall call His name Jesus, for He will save His people from their sins."

I love how the King James Version translates *sozo* in Mark 5:34: "And He said unto her, Daughter, thy faith hath made thee whole." Her body was *made whole*—no longer broken. But her faith in Jesus had also made her whole spiritually. The Holy Spirit put the pieces of her soul back together.

Jesus stopped to talk to Veronica because He wanted her to see that more had happened than a physical healing. She was interested in the temporal fix to her problems. He emphasized the eternal effects of her faith.

Often when I am waiting, I am focused on getting what I want in the here and now. Cure my sickness. Find me a job. *Please* let this cute handbag be on sale. But Jesus is more interested in eternal results. The waiting seems torturous to us, yet God uses it to form our character, strengthen our faith, and draw us closer to Jesus. Any blessing in this world pales in comparison with these eternal things.

In the in-between times of our waiting, Jesus gives us His blessing of peace. We can wait well when we grasp on to promises of His love and the unshakable confidence that He will work out everything for our good. Our Savior grants the tranquility that comes with knowing that He is sitting right beside us, holding our hands in the waiting rooms of life.

Waiting for Relief

Honestly, I never gave much thought to this story about a woman with an issue of blood. The account encompasses only a few verses in the Gospels. Her story is an interruption in the more well-known narrative of Jairus's daughter. Sure, Veronica's healing was impressive, but Jairus's daughter stole the limelight when Jesus raised her from the dead.

Yet, when I think about what it was like to be this woman, I am astounded by this miracle. I can't imagine being sick for twelve years. I can't fathom the weakness and anemia and loneliness she must have experienced for over a decade.

But I do know one woman who can understand Veronica's pain. My mother, Lorna, has not suffered from a bleeding issue, but for more than ten years she has experienced debilitating back pain. And like the New Testament woman, she has visited many doctors and spent a lot of money on many treatments that promise a cure.

At first my mother was able to alleviate the pain through specific exercises and occasional visits to chiropractors and physical therapists. Lorna is infamous for avoiding doctors, so when she went to a neurologist, my siblings and I knew she was desperate.

Mom was diagnosed with spinal stenosis and was sent to a neurosurgeon. Spinal stenosis is the narrowing of the bone channel that contains spinal nerves, or the spinal cord. The surgeon suggested a procedure to clean out the channels and thus decompress the nerves.

This surgery was a disaster. Because of an allergy to the anesthesia used, my mother threw up constantly the first day after the operation (with twenty staples in her back!) and then experienced terrible headaches. When these headaches persisted, doctors realized the dura—the membrane that holds the spinal fluid—had probably been nicked during surgery. Another operation was required to patch the hole and stop the leak of spinal fluid. To allow the patch to heal, my mother then had to lie flat on her back in the hospital for a week.

After she finally recovered from the surgeries, the back pain was diminished and she was able to return to most of her usual activities. However, a few years later, the pain was back. After her experience with surgery, my mother tried to find other answers. One promising option was spinal decompression treatments at a local chiropractic clinic. The advantages of this treatment? No more surgery! Disadvantages? Fifty treatments over ten weeks that cost thousands of dollars—and this for a woman who got physically ill each time she spent more than twenty dollars on herself.

Unfortunately, the chiropractic treatments only decompressed her wallet. Eventually, the pain again became so debilitating that she took the risk of another back surgery. This time a different neurosurgeon fused three vertebrae with screws and rods, giving space to her compressed discs and pinched nerves.

Thankfully, there were no complications, and after a long recovery she had some relief. But after a few years of relative comfort, the pain returned. No longer a candidate for surgery, my mother has tried spinal injections, physical therapy, laser treatments, special healing salves, chiropractic treatments, and acupuncture. She has visited neurologists and pain specialists. She has spent countless hours in the waiting rooms of various medical personnel.

Sometimes Mom's life seems like an endless waiting room. Lorna is a woman of strong faith. She loves to go to church, to study God's Word, and to serve His people. She has prayed for years for relief from her pain. But so far the only answer she has received is "Wait." God has not healed her pain with His miraculous touch or through the healing hands of physicians. Like the bleeding woman in Capernaum, she has tried every cure she knows of and has spent much money without finding a solution to her problem.

But like Veronica, my mother is also drawn to Jesus. She says, "Pain has helped me to focus on God. I had prayed to grow closer to the Lord, and although this is not the path I would have chosen, pain has drawn me into a deeper relationship with Him. I guess sometimes I need to learn the hard way. Pain isn't fun, but it helps me to focus on eternity. When other things are taken away, like your health and the ability to go where you want when you want, you realize that God truly is all you need."

Sometimes we all need to learn "the hard way." When our lives are hurtling at the speed of a bullet train, we might miss the lessons God is teaching. We may rush past Jesus or only casually bump into Him in the crowd. But when we are put into a waiting room and life slows down, we realize how much we need Him. We are drawn to the Great Healer. And even when we do not receive the physical healing we earnestly pray for, we can hear His voice call out, "Daughter." Our hearts can be made whole and we can experience the peace only He can give.

Waiting for God's Goodness

Veronica came to Jesus for healing of a physical ailment. The Lord helped her see that her faith brought even greater gifts—a soul made whole and peace with God.

Often when we first enter a waiting room of life, we draw near to Jesus to simply get the answer we want. The solution to the financial crisis. The resolution to a family conflict. The end to a loved one's addiction.

We are seeking gifts, but He longs to give us His goodness—apart from the temporal gifts. Lamentations 3:25 says, "The LORD is good to those who wait for Him, to the soul who seeks Him." The Father wants us to know that His goodness is not only shown in His healing touch or in His ability to fix painful situations. My mother will tell you that this has been one of the greatest lessons of her waiting-room period. Although she has not received the answer she desires, she has experienced God's goodness. Her relationship with almighty God has progressed from a need for answers to a satisfaction with God Himself.

Andrew Murray wrote:

> He, the Giver, longs to give Himself and to satisfy the soul with His goodness. It is just for this reason that He often withholds the gifts and the time of waiting is made so long. He is constantly seeking to win the heart of His child for Himself. He wishes that we would not only say, when He bestows the gift, "How good is God!" but that long before it comes, and even if it never comes, we should all the time be experiencing: it is good that a man should quietly wait. "The LORD is good unto them that wait for him!"[11]

> Even if the door to what you want never opens in this lifetime, hear the Comforter's voice at another door, saying, "Jesus will see you now."

Waiting draws us to Jesus. So when you are in one of life's waiting rooms and worry and anxiety are sitting in the seats next to you and whispering worst-case scenarios in your ears, push them away and draw near to Jesus. Even if the door to what you want never opens in this lifetime, hear the Comforter's voice at another door, saying, "Jesus will see you now." We may think we are waiting for a husband, a baby, a cure, or a new job, but ultimately what our hearts desire is God. It may take a long time in the waiting room to discover that truth. But the longer the delay, the more we realize *the Lord* is the one we are waiting for.

God's Grace in the Suffering Woman's Story

The woman who suffered for twelve years with bleeding was considered unclean. She knew she needed to draw near to Jesus to be healed. But she was afraid. Afraid she would be reprimanded for touching the great Teacher and making Him unclean.

She didn't need to be fearful. Everyone else in her life was made unclean from her touch. But the opposite happened with Jesus: she was made clean. The Savior of the world cannot be made impure from contact with sin or disease. Instead He cleanses us.

We don't have to be afraid to draw near to Jesus because of our sins, mistakes, and failures. He isn't bothered by our "uncleanness." He simply invites us to come to Him in repentance and faith. His Spirit cleanses us in the waters of Baptism. He heals us of our disease of sin and His blood makes us pure. "Come now, let us reason together, says the Lord: though your sins are like scarlet, they shall be as white as snow; though they are red like crimson, they shall become like wool" (Isaiah 1:18).

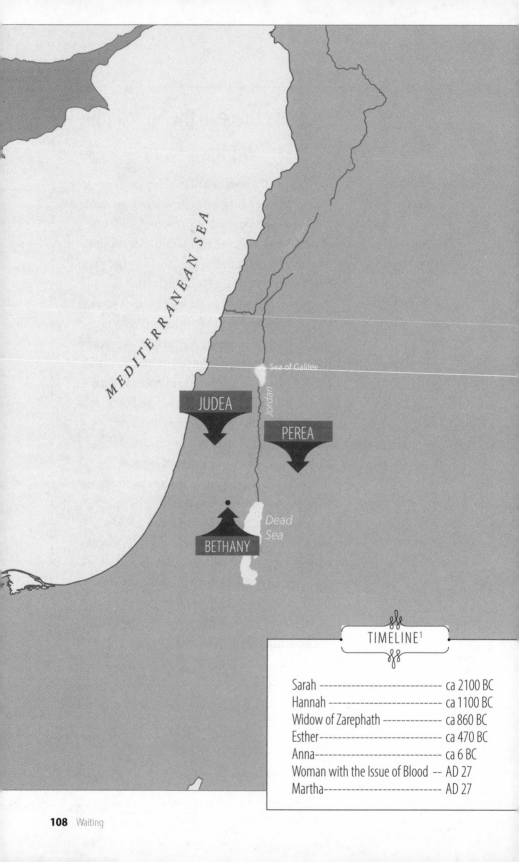

MEDITERRANEAN SEA

Sea of Galilee

Jordan

JUDEA

PEREA

BETHANY

Dead
Sea

Martha

When Waiting Writes a Bigger Story

When I was in college, I hung a poster above my desk where I would see it every day. It was a gorgeous photo of a lighthouse on a rocky cliff. Behind the lighthouse, the sky was filled with bright clouds, as if the sun were trying to make an appearance but was unable to break through the gray curtain. The words on the poster read, "Give God Time."

I bought the poster to remind me that no matter how busy I got with classes and studying and friends, I needed to take time to read God's Word and talk to my Savior. I needed to give God a portion of time each day.

But as I stared at the poster when I was perplexed by writing figured bass for a Bach chorale or when I simply couldn't read another word of Grout's *A History of Western Music*, I realized there was another way to interpret those words. While I was waiting to make friends in this new environment, I needed to give God time. While waiting for guidance, I needed to give God time. While waiting for answers in some challenging relationships, I needed to give God time.

Time to work out everything on *His* schedule.

As I think about this, I am reminded that time is a crucial element in many things. Often time is the most essential ingredient. Take my favorite roasted chicken. The recipe is simple. Make a paste out of olive oil, basil, oregano, and paprika, spread it on a whole chicken, and place it in the slow cooker. Then wait *seven hours* while it cooks on low.

The recipe is simple but torturous. After an hour or two, the whole house is filled with aromas of the herbs and spice and the roasting chicken. As I type away on my computer upstairs, the smell is so enticing that my stomach growls in anticipation. But I know if I sample the chicken before the seven hours in the cooker are completed, it will not only taste terrible, it may make me sick.

Life is like that too. We eagerly anticipate the fulfillment of our dreams: a return to health, restored finances, recovered relationships. But the dream is always out of reach. We seem to have all the necessary ingredients: willingness to work, fervent prayer, deep faith. And yet we wait. Although we're ready to taste and enjoy what our heart longs for, God says we need one more ingredient—time.

God often uses the crucible of time to do spectacular things to fulfill His plans for mankind. When I examine how God worked in the Bible, I see that He frequently didn't work out the answer to the problem right away because delay made the answer that much more miraculous. The birth of Isaac was more remarkable because he was born to a ninety-year-old mother. Joseph's rise to power in Egypt was even more amazing after spending years in prison. The Israelites' possession of the Promised Land was more astounding after being enslaved in Egypt for four hundred years, followed by forty years wandering in a desert—more incredible than if Jacob's descendants had slowly taken over the region. Even though I hate the word *wait*, God seems to love it.

Thinking back to the poster in my college dorm room, I realize that God used the crucible of time to even get me to that place. Years earlier, the desire to study music at the university had seemed an impossible dream, but God asked me to give Him time to work it out. And in the process—in the waiting—God did something bigger than I could even imagine.

In the New Testament, Martha had a similar experience. Time was critical when her brother, Lazarus, was sick. She needed Jesus *now*. But the Teacher waited. She had hoped for a cure for her brother, but Jesus used time to do something more astonishing than she could envision. In the crucible of delay, God worked a marvelous miracle.

Setting the Scene

I can picture Martha in the village of Bethany, pacing the packed dirt floor of the home she shared with her siblings. In my mind's eye, I see her sister, Mary, kneeling by Lazarus's bed, placing a cool cloth on her feverish brother's head. Mary is quiet, but Martha, always a woman of action, can't seem to sit still. She wonders, *What more can I do?* She has already done everything she can think of—including sending a trusted friend to find Jesus. The message to the Teacher was simply, "Lord, the one You love is ill."

Lazarus was not getting better. In fact, his condition was worsening by the hour. Then suddenly, Mary's low murmurings and quiet tears changed into a deep and mournful wail. Martha hurried to her brother's bedside, but it was clear: Lazarus had died.

Jesus hadn't come. Now it was too late.

Where was Jesus? Scripture tells us He was on the other side of the Jordan River in a region called Perea. He had left Jerusalem after the Jews there had attempted to stone Him.

I'm sure that when Martha's friend found Jesus and shared her message, he probably expected the Teacher to immediately follow him to Lazarus's

BETHANY

The village of Bethany was on the eastern slope of the Mount of Olives, about two miles east of Jerusalem. The name can mean either "house of misery" or "house of dates" (the latter presumably because of the date palm trees that grow there).[2]

Bethany is most famous for being the home of Jesus' friends: Mary, Martha, and Lazarus. In fact, the town now bears the name *el-Azariyeh*, or "place of Lazarus".[3]

bedside. After all, Jesus had visited Lazarus and his sisters at their house in Bethany often. Yet, Jesus made no move toward Judea, saying, "Lazarus's sickness won't end in death. It has happened for the glory of God." Jesus stayed where He was.

Finally, after two days, Jesus told His disciples, "Let's go back to Judea." The twelve followers immediately tried to talk Him out of the journey. "But Jesus," they said, "only a few days ago, they tried to kill You. Why go back now?"

Jesus explained that He needed to continue His work while here on earth. And besides, they needed to go now because "Our friend Lazarus has fallen asleep, and I'm going to wake him up."

Oh, the dense disciples! They didn't get it. "But Lord," they protested, "if he's sleeping, he will soon get better." (Subtext: No need to risk Your life and ours if he's just taking a nap.)

Jesus spelled it out for them: "Lazarus is dead. And for your sakes, I'm glad I wasn't there, because now you will believe." I wonder what thoughts went through those puzzled heads at those words; maybe something like *But we believe already!* or *You stayed here for our sakes while Lazarus was dying?* or *If he's dead, why jeopardize our lives?*

Back in Bethany, Mary and Martha were engaged in the Jewish mourning rituals. Friends and family came to console and comfort. Professional mourners were called on to perform somber music and wail loudly. Sadness saturated the home of the sisters like garlic infused the lentil stew the neighbors brought.

It had now been four days since Lazarus died. Four days of weeping. Four days of mourning. Four days of wondering why Jesus had not come. Then someone announced, "The Rabbi is near," and Martha immediately got up and walked down the road to meet Him before He even reached her home. Perhaps it was a brilliant, unclouded day, and even as the sun shone and the birds sang, Martha wondered how the world could be so bright when her own domain appeared so incredibly dark.

When Martha and Jesus met on the road, her first words were "Lord, if You had been here, my brother would not have died. But even now I know that God will give You whatever You ask."

JEWISH BURIAL PRACTICES

When a loved one died in first-century Palestine, survivors needed to take immediate action. Because of the hot climate and Jewish laws prohibiting a dead body from remaining in a city overnight, burial took place the day of death. The body was washed, anointed with spices or balm, and wrapped in linen. Usually the linen was cut in strips, but some archaeological evidence suggests some bodies were wrapped in single cloths.

Friends or relatives carried the body outside the city on a bier. Depending on the wealth of the person, the grave would be dug in the ground and covered with earth and rocks or hewn in a rocky hillside and covered with a large stone.

A procession of people followed the bier to the grave site, weeping and wailing along the way. Mourning continued for seven days after burial. The mourners wept, fasted, sang dirges, and applied ashes to their heads.[4]

Jesus looked Martha in the eye and said, "Your brother will live again."

"I know he will rise again in the resurrection on the Last Day," Martha agreed.

Jesus pressed a little further: "I am the resurrection and the life. Whoever believes in Me, though he die, yet shall he live, and everyone who lives and believes in Me shall never die. Do you believe this?" (John 11:25–26).

Martha's words were never more confident: "Yes, Lord; I believe that You are the Christ, the Son of God, who is coming into the world" (v. 27).

Then Martha went back to the house. Mary needed to see Jesus. Jesus needed to see Mary. Martha privately whispered to her sister that Jesus wanted to see her. Quickly, Mary got up to meet Him on the road. And their friends from Jerusalem, assuming she was going to the tomb, followed her.

When Mary caught up to Jesus, she fell at His feet in the dirt of the road and repeated her sister's words: "Lord, if You had been here, my brother would not have died."

Tears slid down Jesus' cheeks. The great Teacher, known for His calm strength, was overcome by the weeping of His friends. And it was obvious to everyone gathered that Jesus cared a great deal for Lazarus.

Jesus wiped away His tears and asked, "Where have you laid him?" Mary and Martha led Jesus to the tomb. Again the Son of God was deeply moved. Standing before the burial cave hewn out of the rocky hillside, looking at the large boulder covering the entrance to the tomb, Jesus said, "Take away the stone."

Martha protested, telling Jesus that Lazarus had been dead for four days, and saying, "By this time there will be an odor."

"Didn't I tell you that if you believed, you would see the glory of God?" Jesus responded. The stone was rolled away.

Jesus looked up to heaven and began a conversation with His Father: "Father, I thank You that You have heard Me. I knew that You always hear Me, but I said this on account of the people standing around, that they may believe that You sent Me" (John 11:41–42).

Then Jesus called, "Lazarus, come out!"

The onlookers held their collective breath. What would happen? Would they "see the glory of God" as Jesus said, and what would it look like? Surely it was insane to believe someone who had been dead for four days could just get up and walk out of a tomb. But soon, a man came out, hands and feet still wrapped in strips of linen, his face covered by a burial cloth.

Jesus said, "Unbind him, and let him go" (John 11:44).

Jesus Loves Enough to Delay

In that moment, I'm sure the joy of having her brother back erased all of Martha's sadness. But what was she feeling in those days while she was waiting for Jesus to come? And what did she think when it was clear He was not coming as quickly as He could? Those days must have seemed like years.

I know that when life is going according to my plan, it's easy for me to sense God's love. I see His love in the azure-blue sky and the budding pink magnolias. I hear His words of affection in the songs on the Christian radio station and in Sunday's Gospel lesson. I smell it in the scent of the lilacs in my backyard and even in the double chocolate cake baking in my oven. (Surely it was a loving God who created chocolate!)

But when God has pressed the pause button on all my dreams and desires, it's more difficult for me to sense God's abundant love. I become easy prey to Satan's whispers of "Well, God must be really miffed with you. Things have never looked worse. Does He *really* love you?" Instead of breathing in the delicious aroma of God's love, doubt creeps in like the rotten odor of garbage left in the kitchen can too long.

Maybe Martha felt the same way. After all, she and Mary had sent word to Jesus. The messenger probably returned with news that, yes, he had relayed the news of Lazarus's illness. But no, Jesus had not returned with him.

Why had Jesus not come? When the sisters sent the message, they had been confident of Jesus' love. They were so sure of His affection that the message they sent was simply "Lord, he whom You love is ill" (John 11:3). They didn't even include the name "Lazarus." And the Greek word they used for "love" was *phileo*, the love between close friends.

But Jesus didn't come. And Lazarus died. *Yes,* Martha reasoned, *perhaps He could not have reached Bethany before the illness overtook my brother, but He could have healed him with a word.* And now, it had been four days since Lazarus had died. Friends from Jerusalem had come to comfort them and mourn, but the one Friend she desperately needed had stayed away.

If I had been Martha, I would have not only been sad but offended. I probably would have thought, *How many times have I cooked for that smelly bunch of disciples? How many times have I welcomed those ill-mannered followers of Jesus into my home? And now, just when I really need Him . . .*

Perhaps doubt of Jesus' love grew with every minute of waiting. Didn't He love them anymore? Had they done something to make Him angry? Was Jesus judging them for some offense?

But their doubt was pointless. The apostle John wrote, "Now Jesus loved Martha and her sister and Lazarus" (John 11:5).

John is saying, "Now I want you to know, just in case you were wondering, even though it might not look that way, Jesus loved these three friends." And the word he used for "love" here is not *phileo*, the word used for the love of close friends; it is *agapao*, the highest form of love. *Agapao* is the word used to describe God's sacrificial love in sending His only Son to save the world (John 3:16). It's the limitless love the Father has for the Son (John 3:35). It's the servant love Jesus had for His disciples when He washed their feet (John 13:1). The love Jesus had for Martha, for Mary, and for Lazarus was even greater than Martha had imagined.

Delay in answers to our prayers is not a sign of Jesus' lack of love for us. Instead, it may be a sign of His abundant love for us.

Yes, Jesus loved His friends, but then comes the shocker. When I read the next sentence in John's Gospel, my jaw drops to my belly button and I murmur, "Huh?"

"Now Jesus *loved* Martha and her sister and Lazarus. *So,* when He heard that Lazarus was ill, He stayed two days longer in the place where He was" (John 11:5–6, emphasis added).

I say, "What!?! You mean Jesus loved these friends with the same boundless, immense, immeasurable love that He received from God the Father—and *therefore* He didn't go to them right away?"

Yes, that is what John is saying: *because* He loved them, He made them wait.

You might need to read that again and sit with it a moment. I know I did.

Now change that concept a bit and make it more personal: because Jesus loves you with an immeasurable love, He is allowing you to wait. To wait for money to pay the bills. To wait for an answer to the pain. To wait for a prodigal child to return.

God loves us enough to delay in answering our prayers.

This makes no sense to us. This is probably because often we are the spiritual equivalent of the two-year-old in the grocery checkout line screaming for M&M's who can't fathom why his mother would not buy them for him immediately. We can't understand this truth, but Martha's story tells us it is true: Delay in answers to our prayers is not a sign of Jesus' lack of love for us. Instead, it may be a sign of His abundant love for us.

Glory, Faith, and Astonishment

Jesus loves us enough to change us through the painful process of delay. In His hands, delay can make our small lives a conduit for His glory. Delay can be a faith-building exercise. Delay can make God's answers to our prayers more astounding than we can imagine.

Jesus loves us enough to use delay in order to make our problems and predicaments a conduit for His glory. When I was a kid, I loved the fairy tale of Rumpelstiltskin, who was able to spin straw into gold. My mother had an antique spinning wheel in our basement and I thought of how wonderful it would be if I could gather some straw from my uncle's farm and spin it into gold whenever our family needed a little cash. (Family vacation to Disneyland, anyone?)

I never acquired that ability, of course, but Jesus is able to spin all of our troubles into gold, the gold of His glory.

When Jesus heard about Lazarus's illness, the first thing He says is "This illness does not lead to death. It is for the glory of God, so that the Son of God may be glorified through it" (John 11:4). Now, the first thing you might say is, "Wait—Jesus said the illness wouldn't end in death. But Lazarus died." Yes, but he didn't stay dead. The illness didn't *end* in death.

Jesus was able to take the horrible, horrendous, heart-wrenching illness and death of His dear friend and transform it into an opportunity for His power and glory to shine. He took a rotting, stinking corpse and brought it back to life. He grasped on to the darkness of the day and put it through the spinning wheel of His power and love and spun it into the brightest display of His glory.

As I look at that, I think, if God is able to spin glory out of death, maybe I can trust Him to create something beautiful out of the mess of my life. I remind myself that God is in the business of transforming our problems into something that will display His power. He makes a practice of turning sorrow into evidence of His love.

> If God is able to spin glory out of death, maybe I can trust Him to create something beautiful out of the mess of my life.

Of course, I don't imagine that when Martha was waiting for Jesus to show up, she was thinking, *I'm glad Jesus is taking so long to get here. I'm happy He's making us wait. I know this will result in something spectacular.* When we're in the middle of the problem, when the crisis fills our minds, we can all be tempted to feel like Jesus is on the other side of the Jordan and doesn't care enough to come.

But what if we focused on Jesus' ability to spin glory out of pain? What if we reminded ourselves that this illness, this financial crisis, this broken relationship doesn't mean God's love has left the country? Perhaps the dark times wouldn't seem so black. Maybe we would even glimpse signs of God's glory in the darkness.

Jesus loves us enough to use delay as a faith-building exercise. I love the story about Martha and the resurrection of her brother for many reasons. Of course, I rejoice with the two sisters and the rest of the crowd when Lazarus waddles out of the tomb, still bound up in his grave cloths. I cheer, "Yay, Lord!" and applaud Jesus' victory over death. But I also love this story because I am relieved to see that Martha gets some good press. Often this woman of Bethany is only remembered for her worrying and her distracted busyness. The image dialed up on the screens of our minds when we hear the name Martha is that of a woman bustling about in the kitchen, peeling carrots, when she should have been sitting in the living room, listening to Jesus. And the Martha in me relates to her tendency to show love for God in productive action instead of relaxed relationship.

But in John 11, we see another side of Martha. When Jesus met her on the road to Bethany, He gave a clear definition of who He is: "I am the resurrection and the life. Whoever believes in Me, though he die, yet shall he live, and everyone who lives and

WOMEN'S WORK

Martha is often remembered as the one who worked instead of listening. What kind of work did women have to do in an age without Swiffers, dishwashers, and frozen dinners?

Women were busy from morning to night:

hauling water from the nearest well,
grinding grain into flour,
mixing, kneading, and baking the flour into bread,
purchasing meat and vegetables from the market,
preparing the food for meals,
carding, spinning, and weaving threads,
sewing clothing,
washing clothing, and making goods to sell at the marketplace.

In Martha's day, it was especially true that "a woman's work is never done."

CHRIST

When Martha made her bold confession of faith, she said, "Yes, Lord; I believe that You are the Christ, the Son of God, who is coming into the world" (John 11:27). She called Jesus her "Lord," declaring her obedience and submission to His authority. She called Him "the Son of God"—not just a prophet, but Deity in human form.

And Martha called Jesus "the Christ." What exactly does *Christ* mean? The Greek word is *christos* and is equivalent to the Hebrew word *meshiach*, or *Messiah*. Both mean "anointed." Christ—Messiah—is "the Anointed One of God."

In the Old Testament, God appointed people to anoint individuals for specific tasks. Moses anointed Aaron to be high priest. Elijah anointed Elisha to be prophet. Samuel anointed David to be king.

The act of anointing was used most often to confer kingship. This ceremony emphasized the fact that God Himself had chosen the king and given him authority.

In calling Jesus "the Christ," Martha was acknowledging that her dear Friend was the one chosen by God to save her from her sins. He was her King.[5]

believes in Me shall never die" (John 11:25–26). Then He asked her a very pointed question: "Do you believe this?" Martha gave a clear, unwavering statement of faith: "Yes, Lord; I believe that You are the Christ, the Son of God, who is coming into the world" (John 11:27). It makes me want to stand up and shout, "Yay, Martha! You go, girl!"

Martha was more than someone you could turn to when you needed something done. She was someone with rock-solid faith. She may have been busy in the kitchen, but her heart still latched on to Jesus' words.

All the ingredients for faith were there: God's Word spoken through Jesus. A relationship with the Son of God. The Spirit enabling bold confession of belief. Jesus took all those ingredients and used the crucible of time to refine Martha's faith. The waiting deepened her trust.

And Martha's faith was not the only one strengthened. When Jesus announced to the disciples that they were going back to Bethany, He told them, "Lazarus has died, and for your sake I am glad that I was not there, so that you may believe. But let us go to him" (John 11:14–15). Jesus wasn't glad that Lazarus had died, but He rejoiced that this experience would give the disciples' faith an opportunity to grow. By raising a dead man to life, Jesus proved He is the resurrection and the life. He was coming to the end of His earthly ministry, and He knew the disciples would need a resilient faith. His act of raising Lazarus after four days proved He could triumph over death, even His own. This was essential as He now set His face toward Jerusalem.

He is more concerned about our faith than our temporary comfort.

Plus, Jesus' four-day delay allowed time for many people from Jerusalem to come to mourn Lazarus's death. They all had a front-row seat to Christ's most amazing miracle so far. John tells us, "Many of the Jews therefore, who had come with Mary and had seen what He did, believed in Him" (John 11:45). The waiting, although painful for Mary and Martha, meant more people heard Jesus' words, witnessed His divine power over death, and came to faith.

God loves us enough to want us to grow in trust. He is more concerned about our faith than our temporary comfort. And any waiting period we experience may not only be for the sake of our faith, but for the faith of those who watch us patiently endure.

Perhaps right now you're in the crucible of catastrophe. You feel like you have all the ingredients of faith: You hear and believe God's Word. The Holy Spirit is working in your heart. But maybe Jesus knows the missing ingredient is time.

Jesus loves us enough to use delay to answer our prayers in a bigger way than we can imagine. Because Jesus is the omniscient, omnipotent God, the story of Lazarus could have had several different plots. Jesus knows everything about the present and future, so He could have made sure that He was in Bethany when Lazarus became ill. Or if He chose to go to the east side of the Jordan, He could have healed His friend with a word from a distance, like He healed the centurion's servant in Capernaum. Or He could have stayed in the region of Perea but used His power to keep Lazarus alive until He reached Bethany.

But Jesus didn't write the story that way. Because Jesus loved His friends, He stayed where He was so they could witness a bigger miracle, a greater manifestation of His power.

Jesus had already established the fact that He had the power to heal. Stone-deaf ears, unseeing eyes, life-threatening fevers were no match for the Healer. And He had even raised a little girl off her deathbed and brought a widow's son back to life.

But this was different. Lazarus had been dead for *four days*.

> Waiting is a little easier if I remember that God often delays an answer because He wants to do something bigger in my life.

Decomposition had already set in. When Jesus asked that the stone be rolled away, Martha stated the obvious: "Lord, by this time he stinketh" (John 11:39 KJV; I love the quaint wording of the King James Version). Four days was also significant because rabbis of Jesus' day taught that the soul hovered over a dead body for three days before it departed completely.[6] Now at day four, Lazarus was totally, undeniably dead.

Healing Lazarus would have been a wonderful miracle. Raising him off his deathbed would have been astounding. But calling him out of the tomb after four days was jaw-dropping.

Admittedly, I don't necessarily want to hear that God loves me enough to use delay to answer my prayers in a bigger way than I can imagine. Because I hate waiting, I would rather have my prayers answered according to my plan, my timetable. Most of the time, I don't care about waiting well, because I would rather not wait at all. Yes, I admit, God might have a better design for my life. But if that involves a long period of pain and uncertainty, small now instead of great later seems like a much better option.

But when God has placed me in a crucible of delay with no apparent way out, it helps me to remember how He works. Just like my slow-cooker chicken is worth waiting seven hours for, so is God's plan for my life. Waiting is a little easier if I remember that God often delays an answer because He wants to do something bigger in my life. Sometimes this bigger thing is the miraculous transformation of my heart. Maybe the prayer is never answered the way I would like, but God gives a peace and a joy that can only be explained by the power of His Spirit.

The pain of delay can be eased when we expect our waiting times to accomplish something wonderful in God's plan. Waiting well means anticipating something more marvelous than we can imagine.

More Than I Can Imagine

Life is funny sometimes. Just when you think everything is working out according to your chosen recipe, God throws in an unexpected ingredient. Or He removes an item you are convinced is essential to your formula for a joy-filled life.

I can't tell you how many times this has happened to me because God has altered my life recipe more times than I want to count, but I will tell you one story from my high school days when God removed an ingredient I thought was crucial to my happiness.

My Midwest town was fortunate to have a gifted high school choir director. I don't know how he did it, but Mr. Larson turned out amazing choral ensembles year after year. Because I had been studying piano and singing in school choirs from the age of five, I was eager to be a part of one of these talented groups.

Under Mr. Larson's direction, my love for music grew and my abilities developed. Near the end of my sophomore year, Mr. Larson held tryouts for the Concert Choir—the elite large ensemble. Because he was such a talented director, competition was stiff, and I prayed God would give me a spot in this top choir.

However, the day of tryouts, I came down with a cold and the sounds that came out of my mouth were anything but melodious. When the roster of the next Concert Choir was posted on Mr. Larson's door, my name was not on the list.

In typical teenage fashion, I was devastated, not only because my desire to sing in the Concert Choir was shattered, but because my hopes for a future in music were obliterated. I had already been giving some thought to college. I wondered, *Could I turn my love of music into a profession? Could I major in music and become a teacher of the art I love so much?* Mr. Larson seemed to be saying no. If I wasn't talented enough to make a top choir in high school, I was certainly not gifted enough to make a career out of music.

I spent a couple of days crying into my pillow, wondering why God had denied my prayer. Everything in my life so far had seemed to point in the direction of music. Why had God let this happen? Why did He lead me toward a career in music and then pull the rug out from under me?

After a few days of prayer, I realized I had allowed music to become too important in my life. It had taken the number one spot in my heart that only God should occupy. I knew I needed to surrender this dream that had surreptitiously become an idol. Tearfully, I offered it to God. I was ready to give up my ambitions of a musical career, if that was God's will. In effect, I put music in the tomb, and I didn't know if God would resurrect it.

The next few days seemed like years, but then I had an idea. Could I approach Mr. Larson, tell him I had a cold the day of the audition, and ask him for a second chance? As I prayed about it, I sensed no barricades to this idea. Well, Mr. Larson agreed, gave me a new audition, and added my name to the list of Concert Choir members. I was ecstatic.

But the story doesn't end there. What happened next I would never have imagined. As the school year came to a close, a friend from choir approached me and asked me if I would be interested in joining the school band. I'm sure I looked at him like he was crazy. My instrument was piano, and I couldn't picture carrying five hundred pounds of keys and strings on the marching band field. But my friend explained the band director was looking for a new percussionist to play the xylophone, marimba, and bells. He wanted someone

WHEN GOD SAYS NO

Yes. No. Wait. As a child, I was taught these were the three answers God gave to my prayers. We all rejoice when God says yes and we receive exactly what we want when we want it. We grumble and complain when God says wait, but often we see God's wisdom in delay when we finally receive the answer to our prayers.

But what do we do when God says no? Part of my musical ambition as a teenager was to ultimately become a professor at the college level. A variety of circumstances, including our decision to homeschool our children, never made that dream feasible. The answer to that prayer was no.

We all experience the death of desires and dreams. No, your management position will not be reinstated. No, you will not be able to bear children. No, your disease is not curable.

It's easy to offer the trite "When God closes a door, He opens a window." Sometimes that is true. Instead of teaching college students, I had the privilege of teaching my own children. Friends of mine have fostered and adopted children when the door to biological children was closed.

But ultimately, when God says no, we are facing a choice. Will we still trust the Lord? Will we still love Him? Will we be able to say with the prophet Habakkuk, "Though the fig tree should not blossom, nor fruit be on the vines . . . yet I will rejoice in the Lᴏʀᴅ" (Habakkuk 3:17–18)?

A no answer gives us an opportunity to cling to the Lord's goodness apart from His tangible gifts—to relax in God's waiting room, trusting in His wise plan for our lives, confident in His love.

who played the piano and could easily learn these keyboard instruments. I jumped at the opportunity to join another music ensemble.

The next year God surprised me again when I was also invited to join the orchestra as a percussionist and was chosen for the very small, select Chamber Choir. After high school I traveled for a year with the Christian group Joy Inc. And then I was accepted into the university to study music, where every day I was reminded: "Give God Time."

> God had delayed in answering that prayer to work in my heart, but then He gave me more than I had ever imagined.

My prayer as a teenager had been only to be a part of the Concert Choir. God had delayed in answering that prayer to work in my heart, but then He gave me more than I had ever imagined.

This story isn't significant to anyone but me, but maybe you have a similar tale. A dream that died. A desire that glowed for a while but was extinguished. A hope in your heart that seemed to come from God but never happened. Perhaps years have gone by and you now see with hindsight that God did work things out in a bigger way or that the death of the old dreams made way for God's new and better plans for your life.

But maybe you are still waiting. In that case, I pray my story may help you wait in expectation that God is working something out—something better than you imagined. And if years go by and the dream isn't realized, remember that believers in Christ have an eternity to savor God's best.

Awesome Things We Did Not Look For

Imagine a friend invites you over for coffee and dessert. The dining room table is set with lovely quilted place mats and her best white china. As you sit admiring the silver rim on the plates, your friend enters the room with a large silver serving tray. She sets the tray on the table and you look at its contents curiously. It holds a bowl of flour, a measuring cup of sugar, a little dish containing a raw egg, and a glass measuring cup filled with vegetable oil. Your friend takes the chair across the table from you, smiles, and says, "Enjoy!"

You're wondering if stress has sent your friend over the edge. While you're trying to come up with a polite way to decline this feast, she jumps up and laughs, "Oh, silly me, I forgot to mix them together!" Your friend and the tray go back into the kitchen and you hear the whir of an electric mixer. Soon she

> Give God all the ingredients of your life ... and then give Him one more thing: time.

reappears with a large glass bowl filled with what looks like beige-colored soup.[7]

Once again, you try to find a way to graciously refuse. Then your friend sticks her finger in that batter and says, "Well, I guess it does need something else. Maybe if I put it in the oven for a while it would taste better. Would you be willing to wait?"[7]

You agree, and thirty minutes later you taste the lightest, fluffiest cake you could imagine.

God asks us the same question. Our lives are filled with all sorts of confusing ingredients: disappointment, pain, frustrations, fears. We wonder how anything good can come out of these things. But Jesus asks, "Are you willing to wait?"

Isaiah 64:3–4 says:

> When You did awesome things that we did not look for,
>   You came down, the mountains quaked at Your presence.
> From of old no one has heard
>   or perceived by the ear,
> no eye has seen a God besides You,
>   who acts for those who *wait* for Him. (emphasis added).

God accomplishes awesome things we do not look for. He acts for those who *wait* for Him. He says to you and me, "Will you wait for Me? I know it feels like I've forgotten about you. It looks like I haven't shown up on time. You're starting to wonder if I still love you. But let Me assure you. I do. I loved you enough to come to this painful world. I loved you enough to die with nails in My hands and thorns on My head. And I love you enough to give you more than you can imagine. It may not look exactly like what you have planned, but I want to give you My best. Are you willing to wait?"

Give God all the ingredients of your life. Your pain. Your broken dreams. Your weary heart. Your overcrowded schedule. Give them all to Him and then give Him one more thing: time.

God's Grace in Martha's Story

"Jesus wept" (John 11:35). The shortest verse in the Bible appears in the middle of the story of Lazarus's illness, death, and resurrection. Tears flow out of Jesus' eyes after He has met the sorrowful sisters. Jesus saw the despair of all who mourned and was "deeply moved in His spirit and greatly troubled" (John 11:33).

Jesus knew that in only moments, He would call Lazarus out of the tomb and all the tears would dry up like dew on a hot summer day. Yet He felt their pain. The Greek word *embrimaomai,* translated "deeply moved," literally means "to snort with anger." Perhaps Jesus was angry that death had any part in the beautiful world He had created and was furious that His friends had suffered its pain. He commiserated with them.

There is a certain comfort in knowing that Jesus understands our pain and weeps with us in the waiting. Even though He knows the glorious outcome at the end of the painful delay, He feels the ache of our souls because He loves us. He cries at the hurt this world and its sin inflicts.

We can be sure of God's grace and love even as we wait.

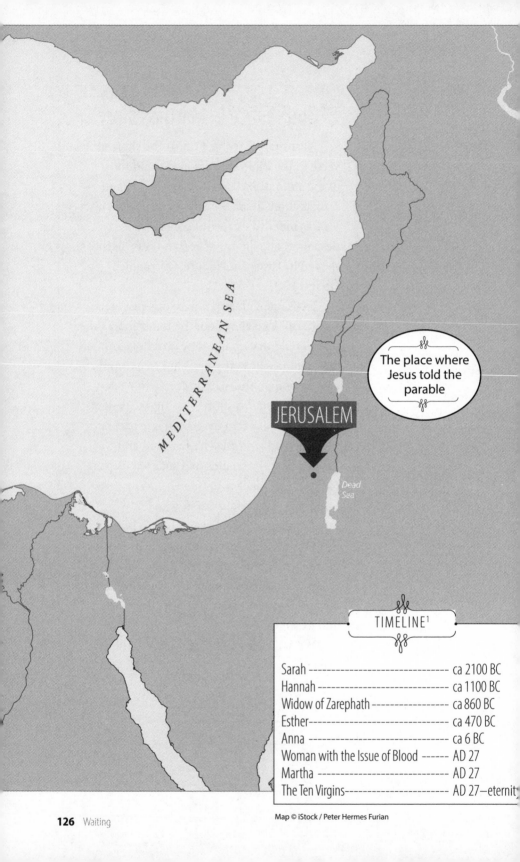

MEDITERRANEAN SEA

JERUSALEM

Dead
Sea

The place where
Jesus told the
parable

TIMELINE[1]

Sarah	ca 2100 BC
Hannah	ca 1100 BC
Widow of Zarephath	ca 860 BC
Esther	ca 470 BC
Anna	ca 6 BC
Woman with the Issue of Blood	AD 27
Martha	AD 27
The Ten Virgins	AD 27—eternity

Chapter 8

The Ten Virgins

It was Christmas Eve, my favorite night of the year.
The balsam fir in the living room was wearing a stunning array
of gold and white ornaments, accessorized with the
jewels of tiny white lights and a sparkling gold garland.

My mother, father, brother, sister, and I had just returned from Christmas Eve services and were settled in comfy chairs near the tree. I have to admit that although the tree was lovely, my twelve-year-old self was definitely more focused on what was under the tree instead of what was on it. Finally, my mother announced it was time to open presents. My siblings and I ripped the wrapping as quickly as we could, anxious to see what was inside. But my father slowly and carefully unwrapped his gifts so the precious paper could be reused. His impatient children cried out, "Hurry up, Dad!" Oddly, Mom seemed a little detached from the excitement. She didn't hurry to unwrap her presents. She didn't exclaim in surprise when the gifts were revealed.

Gradually the pile of still-wrapped gifts grew smaller. Finally, I reached for my gift from Aunt Gladys. I couldn't wait to see what was inside. As my godmother, Aunt Gladys always bought me something special.

As I began to tear at the wrappings, my mother unexpectedly said, "You're going to love it." Now, how did my mother know what was inside? Had she been up to her usual tricks again? Mom was not known for her patience.

Truth be told, most of us struggle with waiting for Christmas. Little kids anticipate the visit from Santa Claus. Parents can't wait to see the joy on their children's faces. Grandparents yearn to have the whole family together under one roof. We long for the celebration of Christ's birth and the joy that accompanies it.

It's with that same kind of longing that we wait for Jesus' return. But unlike Christmas, which appears on the twenty-fifth of December each year, we don't know when Christ will come to earth again. We can't circle number *25* on the calendar and count down the days. We can't light a candle each week and know that when the fourth one is lit, the time will be here.

What do we do when waiting is all there is? How do we wait well when our hearts ache for relief from this broken world? when our souls long to be united with our Savior? when time seems to drag on and on and on . . . ?

Jesus' parable of the ten virgins gives us some guidance when the wait seems too long. Five of the bridesmaids knew how to prepare for the delay. But the other five did not plan ahead. Let's examine how to prepare for the long wait.

Setting the Scene

It was a perfect evening—they all agreed. The moon was almost full. The sky was like the blackest of silk sprinkled with sparkling gems. A gentle breeze ruffled their veils as they sat outside, waiting.

This was no ordinary night. It was the night these ten women had long waited for. Soon the bridegroom would come and escort them to the wedding. They were dressed in their finest clothes and wearing every bit of jewelry they owned. They had taken extra care with their hair, and if any of them had been saving some sweet-smelling nard for a special occasion, this was the time to use it.

Because the sun had already set, each woman had brought a lamp to light her way. Without it, the streets were as black as the tar they used to waterproof their baskets.

LAMPS IN THE ANCIENT WORLD

The ten virgins in Jesus' story brought lamps for the wedding procession. Jesus didn't specify what kind of lamp they used. One common type of lamp used in His time was a small, saucer-shaped vessel with a cover. The domed cover had a hole in the middle for air and for adding oil. In addition, on one side of the cover there was a spout for the wick. This small lamp would not have held enough oil to burn all night.[2]

Another option was a torch made of coarse rags tied to a pole and soaked in oil. This may have been a better choice for an outdoor procession. Trimming these lamps would have meant cutting off charred ends of the rags. The oil would have to be replenished frequently, perhaps as often as every fifteen minutes.[3]

At first, the ten women talked animatedly, anticipating the wedding feast. What clothes would the bridegroom wear? What delicacies would he serve? When would he arrive?

But as the night wore on and the bridegroom still had not come, their conversations slowed. Sentences were punctuated with yawns. Silence between comments grew longer, and after a few hours, there was silence instead of chatter. All ten of the bridesmaids were napping under the starry sky.

Suddenly, at midnight, when they were all in deep sleep, someone cried out, "The bridegroom is near! Come meet him!" A few bridesmaids were immediately alert, nudging others still drowsy with sleep. Soon they were all awake, brushing hair off their faces and fixing their crooked veils.

Most important, they grabbed their lamps. They would need them for the procession to the bridegroom's house where they would enjoy the wedding feast. But as they adjusted the wicks to make them burn brighter, they noticed the lamps were almost out of oil.

Five of the bridesmaids quickly reached for the extra flasks of oil they had brought along. Soon their lamps were burning brightly once again. They stood, ready to meet the bridegroom. When the other five realized they had forgotten a crucial step in preparation for the wedding, they begged their friends, "Please, give us some of your oil."

But those ready for the bridegroom explained, "There isn't enough to go around. You'll have to go buy some for yourselves."

So the five with the flickering lamps set out, walking into the night.

Soon after they had left, the bridegroom arrived. Dressed in a colorful robe, he greeted the other bridesmaids. The five bridesmaids immediately followed him to the house he had prepared. Singing glad songs, they paraded through the dark streets, holding up their lamps.

When they arrived at his home, the bridegroom held open the door and with a sweep of his arm, invited them in. He shut the door and the feast began. Fine wine, delicious food, and joyful laughter were passed around the table again and again.

After a while, a knock at the door interrupted the celebration. Conversations stopped long enough to hear voices on the other side say, "Lord, we're here! Open the door for us!" The bridesmaids recognized the voices of their friends who had gone to buy more oil.

But the bridegroom didn't get up to open the door. Instead, he called out,

"Believe me, I don't even know you."

Waiting for the Bridegroom

Jesus' parable about waiting is centered around a marriage celebration. In His time, weddings were usually held in the evening. Dressed in their finest clothes, the bridegroom and his friends paraded through the streets to the home of the bride, where she and her attendants would be waiting. When the bridegroom arrived, he would escort the whole wedding party to the house he had prepared for his new wife.

When the group arrived at the home, the fathers of the bride and

JEWISH WEDDINGS

In Jesus' time, weddings did not include an elaborate ceremony like we have today, but there were several formal stages to the event.

Betrothal. This first step of marriage was a little like our formal engagements, but instead of a season of dating culminating in the young man going down on one knee and offering a diamond ring, parents usually planned the marriage. A third party arranged the terms of the marriage agreement between the two families. On the day of betrothal, the two families gathered and the negotiator brought the marriage contract for both fathers to sign. The young man would bring something valuable to give to the bride as a pledge of his love.

The marriage itself took place between nine and twelve months after the betrothal ceremony. During this time, the couple were considered legally married, but they could not be alone together. The groom used this time to prepare a home for his future bride.

Wedding Ceremony. On the day of the marriage, the bride would bathe and purify herself, then dress in rich clothing and jewels. Her friends would attend her as she waited for the bridegroom. The bridegroom arrived at the bride's house also dressed in fine clothes and accompanied by friends. They all proceeded to the home he had prepared. A few people would witness the signing of the marriage covenant and the drinking of wine from the common cup.

Marriage Feast. Many more people would be invited to the wedding banquet, which could last as long as seven days. There would be much feasting and dancing. The bridegroom and bride were treated like a king and queen.

bridegroom signed the marriage document. The couple would drink from a common cup to seal the marriage covenant and symbolize the joy of their new life together. This may have taken place under a *chuppah*—a marriage canopy. A grand feast—as elaborate as the family could afford—would follow. Friends and relatives were all invited to celebrate the happy event.[4]

In Scripture, our relationship with God is often compared to a marriage. Jesus is the Groom and His Church is the Bride. Anticipating the marriage feast and the wonderful new life they will have together, the Church eagerly anticipates the arrival of Christ.

In Jesus' story of the ten virgins, the bride doesn't appear. Instead, her attendants take her place. Representing the individual members of the Church, each virgin awaits the appearance of the bridegroom.

All ten of the virgins were waiting. They were longing for the arrival of the bridegroom, yearning for the joyous marriage feast. Each one of us is also waiting. We are like the bridesmaids, yearning and longing for our Bridegroom, Jesus.

But I struggle with waiting. For one thing, it seems too passive. It appears useless.

BRIDE AND BRIDEGROOM

In His Word, God often chose the marriage relationship as a symbol of His relationship with us.

Song of Songs is the story of the passion of a husband and wife, but it also alludes to God's gracious relationship with Israel and foresees the New Testament concept of the Church as Christ's Bride. "I am my beloved's and my beloved is mine; he grazes among the lilies" (Song of Songs 6:3).

Isaiah talks of the joy of the relationship between bridegroom and bride. "For as a young man marries a young woman, so shall your sons marry you, and as the bridegroom rejoices over the bride, so shall your God rejoice over you" (Isaiah 62:5).

Matthew records Jesus comparing Himself to a bridegroom. "And Jesus said to them, 'Can the wedding guests mourn as long as the bridegroom is with them? The days will come when the bridegroom is taken away from them, and then they will fast'" (Matthew 9:15).

Revelation describes heaven and the marriage of Christ and His Bride. "Let us rejoice and exult and give Him the glory, for the marriage of the Lamb has come, and His Bride has made herself ready" (Revelation 19:7).

TIMING IS EVERYTHING	
Jesus told the parable of the ten virgins in the middle of a very busy week.	
Triumphant entry into Jerusalem	(Matthew 21)
Jesus foretells the destruction of the temple and gives signs of the last days	(Matthew 24)
Jesus tells the parables of the ten virgins and the talents	(Matthew 25)
Jesus talks about the final judgment	(Matthew 25)
The Last Supper	(Matthew 26)
Betrayal and arrest	(Matthew 26)
Crucifixion	(Matthew 27)
Resurrection	(Matthew 28)
Jesus knew His time of suffering was drawing near. It was crucial to prepare His followers for the dark days without His presence.	

Because we live in a culture that thrives on achievement and action, some of us have trouble with simply waiting. In fact, as I write this, I am *waiting* in an airport. I could be relaxing. I could be reading the novel in my backpack. I could be engaging in one of my favorite pastimes—people watching. But instead I feel compelled to accomplish something in the hour before my flight. So I sit here at Gate B1, scribbling a few lines.

To me, waiting means there is nothing to do. But as I meditated on Jesus' parable of the ten virgins, I noticed the bridesmaids were doing *exactly* what they were supposed to be doing. Preparing for the bridegroom's arrival *was* their task. Trusting he would show up when all was perfectly prepared *was* their assignment. In our Bridegroom's eyes, waiting is not nothing.

Waiting also seems demeaning. In our society, wealth means having servants and staff who anticipate desires. Status means getting sent to the head of the line. Often, the lower your rank, the longer you wait.

But Jesus' story emphasizes the importance of waiting. The ten virgins were privileged to wait. Just as it is now, there is distinction in being chosen as part of the wedding party. Even though the bridesmaids might have grumbled a bit about the delay, they knew it was an honor to wait for the bridegroom. I need to remember that waiting in hope and love and anticipation of my Bridegroom is a noble task.

Waiting is tedious and tiresome. Jesus' parable emphasized this fact when all the bridesmaids took a nap. But it's important to note that although the ten virgins all grew sleepy, they didn't give up. They dozed, but they didn't abandon their posts. They didn't say, "Well, it looks like this guy isn't coming. Surely this is a sign he's unreliable. Let's all go get something to eat." They stayed out of love for the bridegroom. They knew he was worth waiting for.

When I'm tempted to give up or to invest my energy in something other than waiting for the Bridegroom, I need to remind myself that Jesus is worth every hour, every minute of waiting. The Lover of my soul is on His way. He will whisk me off to the ultimate wedding feast in heaven. By faithfully watching for His return and never doubting His affection, I can demonstrate my love for Him.

Waiting Well

While all ten virgins were waiting for the bridegroom, not all of them were waiting well. Remember that weddings in Jesus' time usually happened in the evening. When the bridegroom arrived and the wedding procession began, they needed lamps to light their way. Plus, the light from the lamps added to the festive nature of the event.

In Jesus' story, all ten of the virgins brought their lamps, but not all were prepared for a long wait. Five of the virgins brought extra oil. The other five didn't think ahead.

Jesus' parable is a warning to all of us that the wait for His return might be longer than we imagine. In Christ's time, many of His followers believed His triumphant return would happen in their generation. But two thousand years later, we are *still* waiting. Discouragement is as plentiful as wine at a wedding. And despair threatens to dim all our lamps of hope.

That's why Jesus explained that we need to be prepared to wait. To wait well, we need to be like the wise virgins who anticipated delay. They brought extra oil to sustain them through the gap in time.

Picture faith as the lamp. The flame burns bright as long as it is supplied with oil. The oil is the Means of Grace—the Word and Sacraments—that sustain faith. Without a continuous source of God's grace, our faith can easily flicker and die out.

Why did five of the virgins not bring the extra supply of oil? Jesus called them foolish. The Greek word, *moro*, means "dull, sluggish, heedless." They didn't plan ahead. They assumed the extra oil would not be needed because the bridegroom would be there soon. Bringing additional fuel seemed like a waste of time. Why bother?

PARABLES

Jesus often spoke in parables. Parables are stories that illustrate a spiritual truth. They teach a lesson by comparing two or more different things, such as the wise and foolish virgins or the religious leaders and the Samaritan.

Parables were told so that only those who cared would come to know the truth. They were the ones who hung around long enough to ask the meaning. The others gave up and left.

The stories Jesus told help us internalize spiritual concepts. They help us understand the kingdom of God and remember sacred truths.

Often I am like one of the foolish virgins. There's no argument that waiting is challenging. When I ask for healing for my husband or when I pray for an opportunity to see my daughter in China, time seems interminably long. When the world seems too painfully broken—beautiful marriages destroyed, innocent children assaulted, good reputations trampled—I long for Christ's return. When I watch the evening news and hear of toddlers killed in inner-city shootings and destruction by terrorists, I cry out, "Come, Lord Jesus!"

And I see myself in the foolish virgins when I try to wait in my own strength. But when I assume extra oil is not needed, I am more likely to listen to the words of Fear. Or stand too long with Impatience and Discouragement. Or spend too much time with Disappointment and Doubt. And they all try to extinguish my flame of faith, or at least keep me too occupied to go to the Source of grace to fuel my trust.

Jesus called the other five women wise. The Greek word here is *phronimos*, meaning "thoughtful and discreet." It implies a cautious character. These women realized the wait could be long. They couldn't rely on only the oil that fit in their lamps. They might need more. So they took the time to go to the source of oil. They bought more so their lamps wouldn't burn out.

I want to be more like the wise virgins who understood that waiting is hard. Who realized that it doesn't take much for faith to sputter and die out. Who recognized that the longer the waiting period is, the more we need the oil of God's grace. I want to wait well like them, prepared for the long haul. You too? Let's all strive to go to the Source often, reaching for the Word to fuel our hope and strength. Let's attend the Lord's Supper to feed our souls.

Jesus told His disciples, "It is the Spirit who gives life; the flesh is no help at all. The words that I have spoken to you are spirit and life" (John 6:63). If we rely on our own strength, our belief may waver. But when we go to the Spirit of life, He reminds us of Christ's words. The flame of faith is sustained; the well of oil is replenished.

Waiting Is Personal

In Jesus' parable, it may seem that the wise virgins were, to put it bluntly, nasty to the other five. They refused to share their oil. They were selfish with their supply.

But they were only doing what they were able to do—direct their friends to the source. We can find the grace that fuels our faith only from God. No one else can give it to us. We can't rely on the faith of our parents to prepare us to meet the Bridegroom. We can't depend on the devotion of our spouse or Christian friends for our own readiness. We must go to the Source—Jesus.

> We can find the grace that fuels our faith only from God. No one else can give it to us.

But we can be like the wise virgins and direct our friends and family to the One who supplies grace and faith. When we notice the people we love neglecting their faith, we can remind them to be ready for the Bridegroom. When their flames are flickering dangerously low, we can point them to the One who refuels their spirits.

READY FOR THE BRIDEGROOM

The foolish virgins weren't ready for the bridegroom because he was delayed. Jesus warned His followers to always be prepared because no one knows when He will return. He said that the faithful "will see the Son of Man coming on the clouds of heaven with power and great glory" (Matthew 24:30). But He warned, "Concerning that day and hour no one knows, not even the angels of heaven, nor the Son, but the Father only" (v. 36).

Another time Jesus instructed, "Watch yourselves lest your hearts be weighed down with dissipation and drunkenness and cares of this life, and that day come upon you suddenly like a trap. For it will come upon all who dwell on the face of the whole earth. But stay awake at all times, praying that you may have strength to escape all these things that are going to take place, and to stand before the Son of Man" (Luke 21:34–36).

Because we can't plan for Christ's return, we need continually go to the source to keep our flames of faith lit. That source is God's Holy Word and Holy Meal, which sustain us just like the oil sustains the lamps of the wise virgins.

We all need to be ready at any time. The bridegroom came at midnight—when all ten virgins were in a deep sleep. No one expected him then. But the wise virgins were ready and were escorted to the wedding banquet. We aren't told if the foolish virgins were able to obtain oil at the midnight hour. But it didn't matter. It was too late.

Wait well by refueling your faith in God's grace.

Waiting for Jesus

I have a love-hate relationship with Advent. As far back as I can remember, I have loved all the preparations of the holiday season. Cookie baking. Present wrapping. Carol singing. But I have always been irritated by the waiting.

In my child eyes, December moved in slow motion. In fact, the closer we got to Christmas, the slower it progressed. Time crept at a glacial pace at the beginning of December. But around December 20, it slowed to the speed of rush-hour traffic in Chicago.

Part of this deceleration of time was due to the arrival of packages. In the weeks leading up to the holidays, friends and godparents would drop off presents with strict instructions: "Don't open until Christmas." The packages teased us, winking at us in their brightly colored papers under the tree.

Aunt Gladys usually arrived with her gift around December 11—my birthday. Kids who have December birthdays know the downside. The birthday is often overlooked in the hustle and bustle of the season. And instead of receiving one present for each event, you may only get one gift "for your birthday and Christmas." But with Aunt Gladys, I didn't mind. It was always obvious she had bought me something really special. She shopped at the best department store in town and had exquisite taste. Getting something from her was a treat for the girl whose wardrobe was made up of whatever was on sale.

Once her gift arrived, it was torture to wait to open it on Christmas Eve. And I wasn't the only impatient one. On Christmas Eve, when my mother said, "You're going to love it," I knew exactly what had happened. Mom had not ignored the winking present. She had peeked inside.

My usually virtuous mother was a repeat offender in one particular crime: package tampering. She had so much practice at gently unwrapping paper and bows and then putting them back together again that you couldn't even tell.

Maybe she should have signed on with the CIA in their stealth operations.

When I finally did open that present from Aunt Gladys, I did indeed love it. It was a navy skirt with pleats. Soft fabric and perfect fit. And best of all, nothing about it said, "Clearance rack." To my twelve-year-old self, it was worth the wait.

Waiting for presents was a grueling test of patience, but even as a child, the longing of Advent was more than yearning for gifts and sugar cookies. I remember attending Advent services and feeling the haunting melody of "O Come, O Come, Emmanuel" weave its way into my soul. The stories of Elizabeth and Zechariah, of Mary and Joseph sank deep into my heart. Each week another candle was lit in the giant Advent wreath that hung from the ceiling of the sanctuary. Another week closer to Christmas. Another step nearer to celebrating the birth of the Savior. Mixed in with the anticipation of gifts was a yearning for Christ.

ADVENT WAITING

Advent is a season of hope and anticipation. The term itself comes from the Latin word *adventus*, meaning "coming." In the Church calendar, the weeks of Advent are a time of expectation. During this time, Christians recall the original waiting by the Israelites for the birth of Christ and look forward to His return.

Advent was not always tied to Christmas. Scholars believe that during the fourth and fifth centuries in Spain and Gaul, Advent was a forty-day period of fasting, penitence, and prayer before the Baptism of new Christians. In the sixth century, Roman Christians began tying Advent to the coming of Christ—but they were thinking of the second coming. Advent was not linked to Christmas until the Middle Ages.

Today Advent means remembering the long wait for Jesus as Savior, and renewing our desire for His triumphant return as King of kings. Seeing the fulfillment of the Old Testament prophecies in the baby in Bethlehem, we are reminded that God is always faithful in keeping His promises. Although we wait with longing, we also wait with confidence.[5]

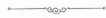

This longing is placed inside each of us. Even though we may receive all the items on our Christmas wish list, we have an ache for something more. We may not be able to articulate the craving in our souls, but we know we are waiting for something better. C. S. Lewis said it this way: "If I find in myself desires which nothing in this world can satisfy, the only logical explanation is

> **We can't do this on our own. We need the oil of God's grace. The fuel of His mercy.**

that I was made for another world."[6]

Perhaps right now you are not waiting for better health or for a more meaningful career. Your family is well and your finances are secure. But you are still waiting. We are all waiting for Jesus.

Our world seems to be falling apart at a faster rate than ever before. The fabric of society is unraveling like the thread of a hem caught in a car door. In just the past two weeks, an extended family member was diagnosed with cancer, a friend told me she was getting a divorce because of her husband's unfaithfulness, and I heard shocking accounts of child abuse in our community. I want to scream, "Lord, stop this! Come now! Come rescue us from this world of pain and loss."

Jesus assures us that He is coming. That there will be an end to this damaged world. That He will come as the Bridegroom and whisk us off to the marriage feast where peace and gladness will be served. Pain and heartache will not even be on the menu.

As part of the Church, the Bride of Christ, we can wait in joy. The moment for celebration is coming. The time when we will be united with the Bridegroom is approaching. We can wait in expectant anticipation. He has promised to come.

But we don't know when He is coming. To wait well, we need to be prepared for delay. We can't do this on our own. We need the oil of God's grace. The fuel of His mercy.

Waiting for Mercy

In the little Book of Jude, I recently found a treasure I hadn't noticed before:

> But you, beloved, building yourselves up in your most holy faith and praying in the Holy Spirit, keep yourselves in the love of God, *waiting for the mercy* of our Lord Jesus Christ that leads to eternal life.
> Jude 20–21, emphasis added

Waiting for mercy. That is what we are all doing. Whatever else we may be waiting for—healing, the proverbial Mr. Right, babies—we are all waiting for the mercy of Christ that leads to eternal life. We are anticipating heaven.

I long for the Bridegroom to come and take me and the rest of the Church to the glorious home He has prepared. A home where we will all be together—no separations from daughters who live on the other side of the world. A home where there will be no pain—my mother's back will be healed. A home where there won't be any sadness—no cancer diagnoses at all.

But how do we wait for mercy?

Remind yourself you are the beloved. Let's back up in the passage. Jude 20 starts out with "But you, beloved." The first step in waiting well is to remind ourselves that we are the beloved. We are the Bride of Christ, showered with a rich, limitless love. When life is hard, it's easy to see yourself as the forgotten, the overlooked, the tossed-aside. But in Christ's eyes, you are always the beloved. While you are waiting, remember the love that compelled the Bridegroom to leave His comfortable, heavenly palace and come to this broken-down world to die for you so He could rescue you.

> When life is hard, it's easy to see yourself as the forgotten, the overlooked, the tossed-aside. But in Christ's eyes, you are always the beloved.

Build yourself up in the most holy faith. Next, Jude instructs his readers to build themselves up in the most holy faith. The verb *building* implies a continuous action. Your faith is not a structure that is assembled and completed, never needing any maintenance. Like a house that needs paint and lamps that need a constant supply of oil, our faith requires an unceasing supply of grace.

> Like a house that needs paint and lamps that need a constant supply of oil, our faith requires an unceasing supply of grace.

I remember a time when my grandfather took the five-hour car trip with my parents to come visit my family and our church. He enjoyed the service, but when it was over, he was ready to leave. Never mind that Bible study was starting; he wanted to go back to the house. Later he asked, "Why the big fuss over Bible study? I learned everything I needed to know in confirmation class. I don't need to go back again." Sadly, many in the Church today have the same view. We don't all see the need for the continual supply of grace to keep our faith flame strong. We don't all turn to the Word for the power to burn brightly.

Pray in the Holy Spirit. Next Jude says, "praying in the Holy Spirit."

Praying is another verb that suggests continuous action. We are to be constantly communicating with God. And when I don't have the words to pray, the Holy Spirit takes over. Romans 8:26 says, "Likewise the Spirit helps us in our weakness. For we do not know what to pray for as we ought, but the Spirit Himself intercedes for us with groanings too deep for words." The Comforter knows my heartaches, my disappointments, my utter weariness and takes them to the Father. He replaces them with the grace to go on.

Keep yourself in the love of God. The word *keep* in the Greek, *tereo*, means "to attend carefully." God's love is always present, but if I'm not paying attention, I may not notice. I might be too busy to hear His voice or too distracted to listen. To keep myself in the love of God is to focus on the loving words of the Bridegroom. Like a World War II bride reading her husband's letters to remind her of his love, read God's love letter often. Just as a soldier's words of affection eased his wife's wait for his return, Christ's promises of love fuel our hearts in the days, months, or years before He comes back.

Tereo can also mean "guard." I need to guard against Satan's deceptions. The deceiver knows that I am in the love of God, but he will do anything he can to make me doubt that fact. He may try to tell me that God's love is dependent on my performance, my achievements, or my goodness. I need to ask the Spirit to guard my heart, strengthen my faith, and help me ignore the lies.

Wait for the mercy of the Lord Jesus Christ. Waiting seems uncertain. What if what I'm waiting for doesn't happen? What if the illness isn't healed? the new job doesn't come through? the relationship remains broken? It's true that the things I desire on earth may never be mine, but the mercy of the Lord Jesus Christ is a sure thing. In the Greek, the word *wait* is *prosdechomai*, meaning "to expect." I don't wait for the *possibility* of mercy; I can *expect* the fulfillment of Christ's promises. Ephesians 2:4–5 tells us, "But God, being rich in mercy, because of the great love with which He loved us, even when we were dead in our trespasses, made us alive together with Christ—by grace you have been saved." Because of Christ's sacrifice, not because of our own actions, we can expect God's mercy to allow us into the wedding feast.

What do we do when waiting is all there is? when our hearts ache for relief from this broken world? when our souls long to be united with our Savior? when time seems to drag on and on and on?

We can try to wait in our own strength. But most of us are like my mom, unwrapping packages that say, "Don't open until Christmas." Our patience is in limited supply. We become like the foolish virgins' lamps. Our faith grows dim and sputters.

Or we can wait in the oil of God's grace. Waiting well is difficult. We can't do it on our own. But we can return to the Source for a fresh supply of grace daily, hourly. He will give us the strength to persevere. He will provide the hope to continue. He will fill us with the assurance of His love. And He will provide us with the sustenance we need in His Holy Meal.

God's Grace in the Parable of the Ten Virgins

Jesus told the parable of the ten virgins to emphasize the fact that each of us needs to be ready for His coming. We all need to prepare for the arrival of the Bridegroom.

Bridesmaids in Jesus' time had many preparations to make. They needed to bathe and purify themselves. A festive occasion like this required a beautiful robe. They had to remember their lamps and go to the market to buy extra oil. All this required specific effort.

Jesus warned us to be ready for His coming, but thankfully, He does all the work. He washes His Bride, the Church, "that He might sanctify her, having cleansed her by the washing of water with the word" (Ephesians 5:26). He provides the wedding dress, clothing us with "the garments of salvation" (Isaiah 61:10). He gives us the "oil of gladness" (Isaiah 61:3), and He Himself is the "light of the world" (John 8:12) to "guide our feet into the way of peace" (Luke 1:79).

Waiting Well

Epilogue

I once read that waiting is the best and truest way to know God. Honestly, that was not something I wanted to hear. As a woman of action, I'd rather pursue God with a list of ten easy steps or a strategic monthly plan.

However, I have to admit that my doing sometimes gets in the way of my relationship with God. My busy-ness prevents me from spending time with Him. My strategic plans block my view of what He has in mind for my life.

In order to draw me closer to Him, God has often enrolled me in a course of waiting. Unfortunately, this has not guaranteed a stronger relationship with Him. Because I often refused to slow down enough to hear His voice, I have not always benefited from these classes.

It's obvious that waiting does not automatically enable us to know God better. But *waiting well* can.

Through the pages of this book, we have read eight stories of women who waited. Through these accounts, we learned what it means to wait well. In the process, we also became better acquainted with God.

Sarah's story taught us that God is worthy of our trust—even when the wait is long. Through Hannah, we learned that while we are waiting, God invites us to relinquish our desires into His loving hands. We were reminded of God's faithful provision through the widow of Zarephath and her daily waiting. Esther's story demonstrated how God is always working behind the scenes, even if we cannot see it.

The short biblical account of Anna helped us see that God has a purpose for each of our lives. Reading about the woman who waited twelve years for healing reassured us that Jesus invites us to come to Him while we are waiting and that He will always give us His undivided attention, no matter how insignificant we feel. When we've waited so long that we begin to wonder if God has forgotten us or ceased to love us, Martha's story reassures us of Christ's *agapao* love for us and His ability to do more than we can imagine. The parable of the ten virgins reminded us that, on our own, we lack the ability to wait well, but that God is always willing to give us more of His grace to fuel our faith.

These women inspire me to wait well. Instead of griping about the in-between times God has allowed in my life, I want to be still long enough to hear His voice. Instead of frantically looking to drop out of the waiting seminar God has enrolled me in, I want to learn the lessons He has in mind.

When we find ourselves in one of God's waiting classrooms, may we wait well by accepting the time to slow down and be still. May we embrace lessons in humility and learn unceasing dependence on a loving Father. May we allow Him to draw us near and receive His grace.

I haven't always waited well, but I've been through enough waiting sessions to learn a few things: God's love never fails. His way is always best. He is always present.

And He is never late.

Study Guide

I invite you to learn more about waiting well and to get to know the eight ladies-in-waiting better by delving into the pages of Scripture. The study questions that follow will help you go deeper into each story. The questions are organized in levels. These are not levels of difficulty but of time.

LEVEL 1: Reflect on the Reading: If you only have fifteen minutes, complete this section. These questions are designed to help you ponder the chapter's lessons and reflect on how the principles learned apply to your life. If you are doing the study in a group, these questions will also help get conversation flowing.

LEVEL 2: Dig into Scripture: If you have more time, you are encouraged to go deeper by reading the Bible story and related passages.

LEVEL 3: Apply the Story to Your Life: At this level, you will take a little more time to discover how the principles of waiting can be used in your ordinary days.

LEVEL 4: Complete a Project: These activities will help you internalize what you learned. You will experience the knowledge in new ways through art, music, and hands-on activities.

To get the most out of this study, I encourage you to complete all the levels. But I realize life is hectic—do what you can.

If you are exploring *Waiting: A Bible Study on Patience, Hope, and Trust* with a group, the leader can choose which questions to discuss and perhaps choose one project to complete together. The study is designed to be completed in eight weeks, but if your meeting time is short, you may want to take two weeks for each chapter. The first week you could discuss the chapter and the "Reflect on the Reading" questions. The second week could be spent on the other three sections of the study guide. (You may also want to wrap up the study by taking an extra week to discuss the Epilogue and questions 2 and 3 of chapter 8.)

However you proceed, may the study questions help you explore God's faithfulness to you—in the meantime. May the Lord's promises increase your trust in Him—even in delay. May time in God's Word strengthen your faith— so that your time is spent waiting well.

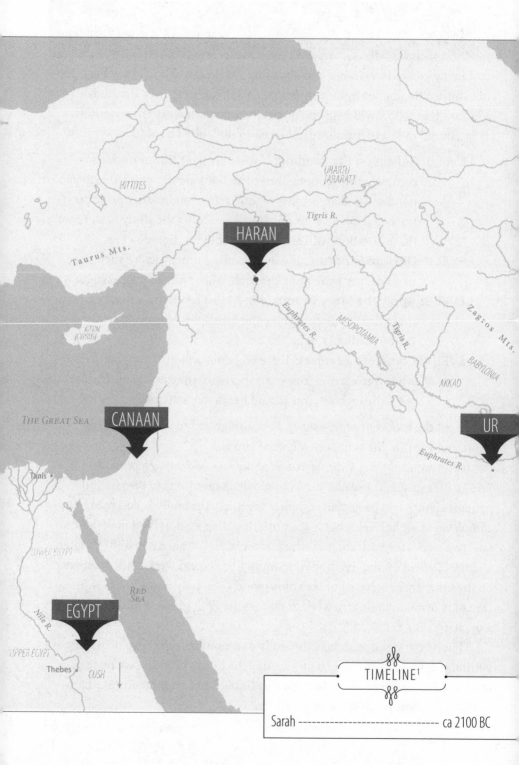

URARTU
[ARARAT]

HITTITES

Tigris R.

HARAN

Taurus Mts.

Euphrates R.

MESOPOTAMIA

Tigris R.

Zagros Mts.

KITIM
[CYPRUS]

BABYLONIA

AKKAD

THE GREAT SEA

CANAAN

UR

Euphrates R.

Tanis

LOWER EGYPT

RED
SEA

Nile R.

EGYPT

UPPER EGYPT

Thebes

CUSH

TIMELINE[1]

Sarah -------------------------------- ca 2100 BC

Sarah

Chapter 1
STUDY QUESTIONS

Level 1: Reflect on the Reading

1. What do-it-yourself projects have you attempted in your life? Which were successful? Are there any you regret?

2. What new insight did you learn about Sarah in the reading?

3. If you were to grade Sarah's waiting report card, what grade would you give her? What comments might you add to her report card?

4. Sarah demonstrated her need to be in control of her life by trying a DIY project. How did God reveal He was the one in control?

5. What was the most important thing you learned about waiting well in this chapter?

Sarah and Abraham's story is spread out from Genesis 11:27–25:11. We will examine the portions most pertinent to Sarah.

1. Read Genesis 12:1–9 and 1 Peter 3:5–6.

    a. How do these two passages relate?

    b. What positive quality does Sarah demonstrate here?

    c. What is God's promise to Abraham here?

2. Read Genesis 15, the story of the covenant between God and Abram.

    a. How does God's promise become more specific here (v. 5)?

    b. Whose name is conspicuously absent from the promise?

    c. How does God demonstrate His power to fulfill the promise?

3. Read Genesis 16.

    a. What character qualities does Sarai demonstrate in this passage?

    b. Why do you suppose Abram agreed to Sarai's DIY plan?

    c. How did the plan backfire?

4. Read Genesis 17:1–8, 15–21. How did God's promise become more specific here?

5. Read Genesis 18:1–15.

    a. Is there anything about God's promise here that is different from the one He gave in Genesis 17?

    b. Why do you think God repeated the promise?

    c. What does Sarah's laughter reveal about her character?

    d. What other character qualities do you see here?

6. Read Genesis 21:1–7.

    a. How is Sarah's laughter different here?

    b. How would you describe her character now?

7. Read Hebrews 11:11. What is Sarah's predominant character quality here?

8. Summarize what you learned about Sarah's character by completing this chart:

Scripture	Sarah's Character Qualities
Genesis 12:1–9 and 1 Peter 3:5–6	
Genesis 16	
Genesis 18:1–15	
Genesis 21:1–7	
Hebrews 11:11	

9. Look over this "Dig into Scripture" section and examine the promises God made to Abraham over time.

    a. Why do you think God revealed a bit more detail each time He spoke with Abraham?

    b. How does this relate to God's command to Abram in Genesis 12:1: "Go from your country and your kindred and your father's house to the land that I will show you"?

    c. How does Abraham's experience with both God's command and promises help you when you feel like God has not given you much in the way of life direction?

Level 3: Apply Sarah's Story to Your Life

1. Review the character qualities Sarah demonstrated. Which ones are evident in your life? Choose one of the positive qualities to nurture or one of the negative qualities to banish. What is one thing you could do this week to make that happen?

2. When Abram and Sarai were in Haran, they were in an in-between place. They had left their old life, but they were not where God ultimately wanted them.

    a. When have you felt that you were in an in-between place?

    b. It seems Abram's in-between place came because of incomplete obedience to God's command. If you are in an in-between place now, do you think God is asking you to step out in faith and obey in a new way? Explain.

3. When God made the covenant with Abram in Genesis 15, Abram was sleeping during the most important part, demonstrating that God was the one who would act. Where in your life is God asking you to let go and let Him work?

4. Hebrews 11:11 says, "By faith Sarah herself received power to conceive, even when she was past the age, since she considered Him faithful who had promised." In this passage, only Sarah's faith is mentioned. God seemingly forgot all about her conniving DIY projects and doubtful laughter. How does that encourage you?

Level 4: Complete a Project

1. When Sarah tried her DIY project, she was acting out of self-reliance instead of trust in God's adequacy.

   In what areas of life is it easy for you to trust God's sufficiency? Which areas are difficult? Rate each area (1 being the easiest to trust God's sufficiency up to 5 being the most difficult):

   Family

   Friends

   Work

   Spiritual life

   Health

   Finances

   Write a prayer asking God to help you trust Him in your most difficult area.

2. The big lesson God wanted to teach Sarah was "Nothing is too hard for the Lord."

    a. How would Sarah's life have changed if she had believed that?

    b. How would your life change if that became less of an intellectual fact and more of a guiding life principle?

    c. Using a 3 × 5 card or a piece of plain paper along with colored pencils or markers, create an artistic version of the words of Genesis 18:14: "Is anything too hard for the LORD?" Start by choosing one color for the word "anything" and another for "LORD." Write these in large letters. Then, using a black pencil or marker, write the rest of the words around these two words. Doodle pictures or symbols of things for which you are having trouble trusting God. While you are writing, ask God to give you faith in these areas.

3. In Genesis 15, God appeared to Abram in the form of a smoking fire pot and a blazing torch. Light a candle as a symbol of God's presence with you. Thank Him that He is always with you, always working for your good. Ask Him to give you faith to trust His timing in your life.

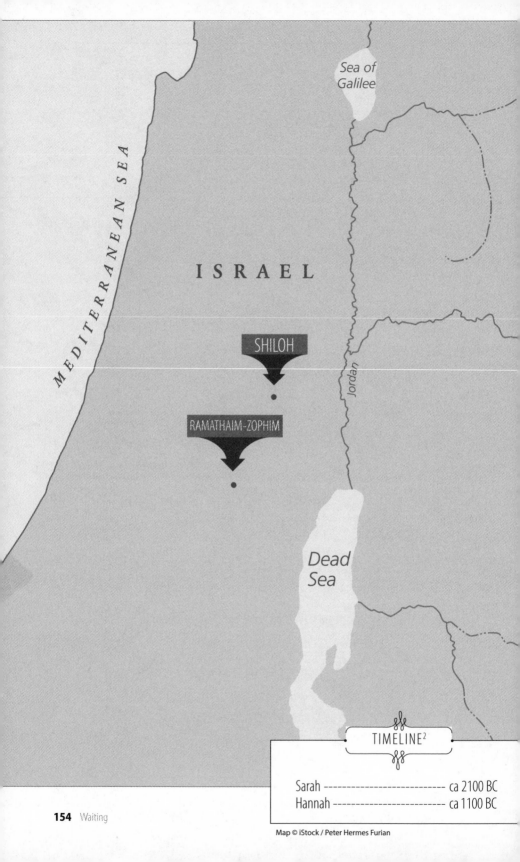

Sea of
Galilee

M E D I T E R R A N E A N   S E A

I S R A E L

SHILOH

RAMATHAIM-ZOPHIM

Jordan

Dead
Sea

TIMELINE²

Sarah ---------------------------- ca 2100 BC
Hannah ---------------------------- ca 1100 BC

Map © iStock / Peter Hermes Furian

Hannah

Level 1: Reflect on the Reading

1. Describe your emotions when you are waiting in line.

2. What new insight did you learn about Hannah in the reading?

3. If you were to grade Hannah's waiting report card, what grade would you give her? What comments might you add to her report card?

4. In chapter 1, we studied the life of Sarah. Both Sarah and Hannah were living in similar circumstances. Compare and contrast how these two women handled their long waiting periods.

5. What was the most important thing you learned about waiting well in this chapter?

Level 2: Dig into Scripture

Read Hannah's story in 1 Samuel 1:1–2:21.

1. Sacrifice is a major theme in Hannah's story.

   a. This section of text contains an *inclusio*. Review what this term means on page 32 and write out the meaning here.

   b. What word appears in both 1 Samuel 1:3 and 1 Samuel 2:19 that highlights the theme of this section?

   c. Now look at Hannah's words in 1 Samuel 1:11, 28. Write out her words of sacrifice found in these verses.

   d. How does Hannah's sacrifice differ from the sacrifices given by the Israelite community in 1 Samuel 1:3?

   e. What sacrifices do you participate in with your worship community? What personal sacrifices have you given to the Lord?

   Sacrifice with my community

   Personal sacrifices

2. Read the following Scriptures and record the kind of sacrifices God desires.

   a. Psalm 4:5

   b. Psalm 50:14

   c. Psalm 51:17

d. Psalm 141:2

e. Which of these sacrifices is God asking you to give today?

3. Reread Hannah's prayer in 1 Samuel 1:11.

   a. What name does she use for God, and what does this demonstrate about her view of God?

   b. What are some of the other characteristics of her prayer?

4. Scripture gives us a vivid picture of Hannah's emotions.

   a. What emotions does she demonstrate in 1 Samuel 1:10?

   b. What are her feelings in 1 Samuel 1:18?

   c. How can you explain the difference?

   d. How would your life be different if you let go of the one thing you are waiting for?

5. When Hannah brought Samuel to live at the tabernacle with Eli, she spoke a beautiful prayer that is sometimes called "the Magnificat of the Old Testament" (1 Samuel 2:1–10).

   a. What gives Hannah joy (1 Samuel 2:1)?

   b. Why is that fact significant at this moment in her life?

Level 3: Apply Hannah's Story to Your Life

1. Hannah was barren for many years. We all face times of barrenness in our work, relationships, or ministry. When have you experienced barren times? Are you facing desolate or empty times right now? In what way?

2. Peninnah is definitely an example of what *not* to do when someone in your life is hurting. Brainstorm some ways you could help someone who has been waiting in line for a long time for an answer to prayer (e.g., send her an encouraging card, tell her a promise of God that has strengthened you during a long wait).

3. Describe your reaction to this statement: Sometimes the longer we stand in line, the more we realize that God is not only the one waiting with us; He is the one we are waiting for.

Level 4: Complete a Project

1. In our readings in 1 Samuel, the people of Israel came to Shiloh to offer sacrifices on the altar. Hannah surrendered her desire for children. Is God asking you to surrender something near and dear to your heart? something that is getting in the way of your relationship with Him? a deep desire that has never been fulfilled? Draw a picture of an altar and then draw what you feel God is asking you to sacrifice today. Then write a prayer, giving it to the One who loves and cares for you.

2. Sing "Take My Life and Let It Be" or listen to "My Heart Is Yours" by Kristian Stanfill (you can find it on YouTube). Inspired by these songs, dedicate your life, your will, your all to the Father who loves you and cares for you.

3. With your group, discuss the attributes of God that Hannah mentions in her prayer in 1 Samuel 2:1–10. Make a poster with pictures or words that depict these characteristics. As you add each attribute, talk about what that characteristic of God means to you personally.

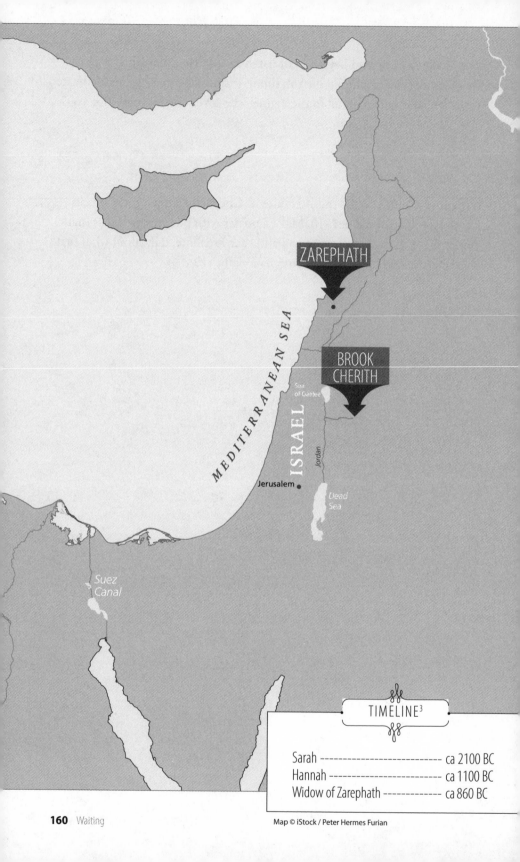

ZAREPHATH

BROOK
CHERITH

Sea
of Galilee

MEDITERRANEAN SEA

ISRAEL

Jordan

Jerusalem

*Dead
Sea*

*Suez
Canal*

TIMELINE[3]

Sarah ---------------------------- ca 2100 BC
Hannah --------------------------- ca 1100 BC
Widow of Zarephath ------------- ca 860 BC

Map © iStock / Peter Hermes Furian

The Widow of Zarephath

Level 1: Reflect on the Reading

1. What is on your to-do list this week?

2. When God places you in a season of waiting, do you view it as a God-ordained mission or as a situation to be endured? Why?

3. If you were to grade the widow of Zarephath's waiting report card, what grade would you give her? What comments might you add to her report card?

4. Describe what might have been going through your head if you were the widow of Zarephath and a stranger asked you to give him your last morsel of food in exchange for an unending supply.

5. What was the most important thing you learned about waiting well in this chapter?

1. Read 1 Kings 17:1–6.

    a. What happens in this passage? How does it set the scene for the widow of Zarephath's story?

    b. The name *Elijah* means "The Lord is my God." How is this significant to the story?

    c. What is unusual about the way God provided for Elijah here?

    d. When has God provided for you in an unusual way?

2. Read 1 Kings 17:7–16.

    a. Why is it surprising that God sends Elijah to Zarephath?

    b. What is your opinion? Do you think the widow's words in verse 12, "As the LORD your God lives," indicate faith in the true God or simply a recognition of Elijah's God? Why do you say that?

    c. God provides for Elijah and the widow here in 1 Kings 17. Look up the following passages and write what God provided and how often.

Passage	What God Provided	How Often God Provided
1 Kings 17:15–16		
Exodus 16:15–21, 31		
Matthew 6:11		

d. Why do you think God emphasized the daily-ness of His provision in these passages?

e. The widow was asked to take a step of faith in order to receive God's promise of provision. Has God ever asked you to take a step of faith that seemed too big—too risky?

f. 1 Kings 17:8 tells us that the Word of the Lord came to Elijah. What was this Word (v. 9)? How does Elijah respond?

g. How does the Word of the Lord come to us today? What is your response to His Word?

3. Read 1 Kings 17:17–24.

    a. The widow and Elijah had different reactions to the tragedy of the death of the boy. Fill out the first two lines of this chart based on the Bible passage.

Person	Response to Tragedy
Widow	
Elijah	
Me	

Each of us also responds differently to crisis. On the third line of the chart above, write down your usual response to tragedy.

    b. What can we learn from Elijah's response?

1. The widow of Zarephath and Elijah lived through three and a half years of no rain. Are you experiencing a kind of drought in your life? A drought of income? A drought of friends? A drought of happiness? How does the widow's story encourage you?

2. When Elijah told the widow to make her last morsel of food and give it to him, he said, "Do not fear." That would have seemed impossible if he had not added God's promise for continual provision (1 Kings 17:13–14). God's Word offers promises for all of us. Look up the following verses and match them with what God promises to provide.

Promise:	What God Provides
____ Deuteronomy 31:8	a. guidance
____ Isaiah 26:3	b. food and drink
____ Isaiah 58:11	c. comfort
____ Jeremiah 31:3	d. love
____ Micah 7:18–19	e. peace
____ Matthew 6:31–33	f. His presence
____ 2 Corinthians 1:3–4	g. forgiveness
____ James 1:5	h. wisdom

What promise do you most need today? In the margin of your Bible or on a 3 × 5 card, make an artistic rendering of that verse. Reflect on the verse, choosing the words that are most meaningful to you. Then write the verse using colored pencils, making those special words larger or in fancier lettering. As you write and draw, pray the words over and over, letting them sink into your heart.

3. In chapter 3, we read, "Each day of waiting is another twenty-four hours to watch Him provide for us in miraculous ways." This week, keep a running list of all the things God provides for you—both big and small.

4. Look up Hosea 12:6 and write it in the form of a prayer. Pray this prayer every day this week.

5. What can you do to develop a *habit* of waiting? What specific things could you do to help you remember to wait on the Lord day by day?

Level 4: Complete a Project

1. Make a simple cake of bread like the widow of Zarephath made every day. (You don't have to use a camp oven or clay oven, though. You are allowed to use your modern range.)

   1 c. whole wheat flour (extra for dusting)

   2 tbsp. extra virgin olive oil

   ½ c. water

   Preheat oven to 350°. Combine ingredients. Knead dough on floured surface for 5 minutes. Roll out dough to about 1/8 inch thick. Place on a cookie sheet that is well oiled or lined with baker's parchment. Bake for 20 minutes.

2. Each day this week, ask God, "What is the one thing You want me to do to-day?" At the end of the week, reflect on how asking that question changed your activities and your stress levels.

3. Has God placed you in a Zarephath right now—a place of waiting? Remember *Zarephath* means "smelting place." How might God want to refine your faith in this time of delay? What might He want to filter out of your life?

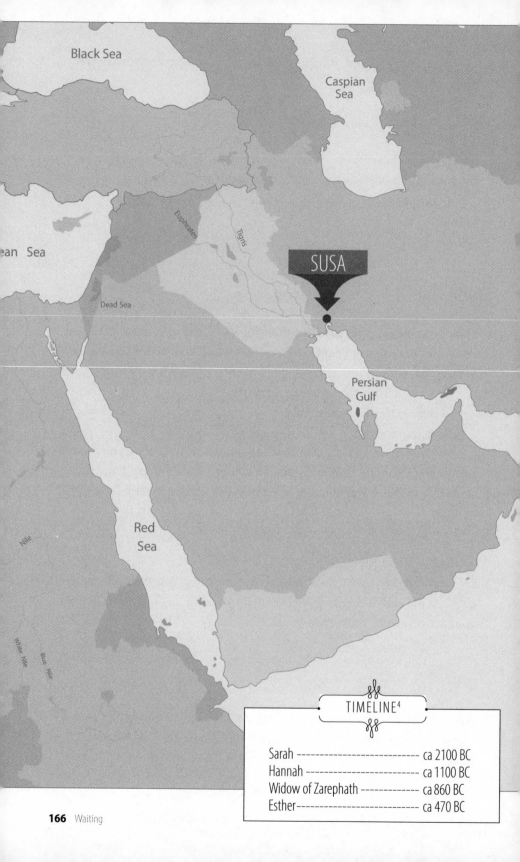

Black Sea

Caspian Sea

ean Sea

Euphrates

Tigris

SUSA

Dead Sea

Gulf of Suez

Persian Gulf

Nile

Red Sea

White Nile

Blue Nile

TIMELINE[4]

Sarah ---------------------------- ca 2100 BC
Hannah --------------------------- ca 1100 BC
Widow of Zarephath ------------- ca 860 BC
Esther ---------------------------- ca 470 BC

Esther

Level 1: Reflect on the Reading

1. When have you experienced delay in your travels? Describe your reaction to layovers, schedule changes, and traffic jams.

2. What new insight did you learn about Esther from the reading?

3. If you were to grade Esther's waiting report card, what grade would you give her? What comments might you write on her report card?

4. Describe your reaction to this statement from the reading: "Perhaps the most frustrating aspect of . . . waiting is that we're stuck in a place where we can't fix the situation on our own or carry out a solution." Do you agree? disagree? Why?

5. What was the most important thing you learned about waiting well in this chapter?

Esther's story is recorded in the ten chapters of the book named for her. We study portions of the Book of Esther here, but you might want to read the whole book. It's the kind of story that would play well on any big screen!

1. Read Esther 2:1–18.

    a. Why might Esther have been happy at being chosen to be part of the search for a new queen? Why might she have been unhappy?

    b. Esther 2:15 says, "Now Esther was winning favor in the eyes of all who saw her." What attitudes and/or behaviors do you think she exhibited to win that favor?

    c. Now consider your own waiting situations. How can you use Esther's example to help you while you wait?

2. Read Esther 4.

    a. In Esther 4:14, Mordecai asks Esther an important question. Write the question here.

    b. What do you suppose Mordecai meant by that question?

    c. Imagine a close friend asking you a similar question: "And who knows but that all your waiting has prepared you for such a time as this?" How would you react? Is it encouraging to think that all your waiting might be preparing you for God's purpose?

    d. What does Mordecai tell Esther will happen if she keeps silent (v. 14)?

e. Mordecai's statement in 4:14 is the clearest declaration of God's providence in the Book of Esther. His words imply that if Esther doesn't act, God will work through other means. (Note: Mordecai's words about her safety are not a threat but a word about the true danger ahead.) If God can do His will without us, why should we bother to obey when there is personal risk to do so?

f. When Mordecai asked Esther to go to the king and plead for her people, she did not go immediately. What did she do instead (vv. 15–16)?

g. What can we learn from Esther's example here?

3. Read Esther 5:1–8. Some commentators think the Hebrew construction of verse 7 indicates Esther started to state the request to save her people, "My wish and my request is:" but she paused and changed course: "let the king and Haman come to the feast . . . tomorrow." It seems likely that the Holy Spirit prompted her to delay her appeal. When has God prompted you to wait? Or how may God be asking you to purposely pause right now?

4. Read Esther 6.

   a. How is God's providence demonstrated in the events of that night?

   b. Esther might have been fast asleep while all this was happening, or she might have been on her knees, asking for the right words for the king. In any case, Esther did not have anything to do with all the "coincidences" that occurred in the time between her banquets. How does this encourage you?

5. Read Esther 7.

    a. How would you describe Esther's words when she finally states her request (vv. 3–4)?

    b. You might have included "humble" in your description above. What are some other ways we see Esther's humility in the Book of Esther?

    c. Why is humility an important attitude to have when we are in a waiting period?

Level 3: Apply Esther's Story to Your Life

1. Do you feel like you are stuck in Death Valley? If you are in a desert of delay, how can you use the four steps spelled out by the word *PRAY*? Name some specific actions you can take. (If you aren't stuck in a waiting desert right now, consider how yvou could use the steps in the future.)

    Prepare for what is coming.

    Rest in God's providence.

    Ask God for the next step.

Yield to God's sovereignty.

2. When we are waiting, we want God to remove all the roadblocks on the itinerary we have chosen. How could roadblocks be a blessing?

3. Psalm 27:14 tells us, "Wait for the LORD; be strong, and let your heart take courage; wait for the LORD!"

   a. What does courage in waiting look like?

   b. Write a prayer asking God to help you have courage in waiting.

Level 4: Complete a Project

1. One of the themes of the Book of Esther is the providence of God—how He works behind the scenes of our lives.

   a. Using the timeline below, write down evidence of God's providence in each chapter. (For example, chapter 1: Queen Vashti refuses to appear, making way for a new queen.)

---

chapter 1   chapter 2   chapter 3   chapter 4   chapter 5   chapter 6   chapter 7

b. Where have you seen the providence of God at work in your life? Did you meet your future spouse "by accident"? Was there a series of "coincidences" that led to the job you now hold? Did you move to a different city and meet your new best friend by "pure chance"? Make a timeline of the evidence of God's providence in your life. (Consider recording both of these timelines in your Bible in the margins of the Book of Esther.)

Personal Timeline

2. Listen to songs about God's providence. Search YouTube for Christy Nockels's "You Are Able" or Hillsong's "Desert Song." Or listen to timeless hymns like "Guide Me, O Thou Great Jehovah" or "My Shepherd Will Supply My Need."

3. Make Hamantaschen. These triangular cookies are traditionally served at the Feast of Purim. The pastries symbolize the hated enemy of the Jews who was defeated. In German, *Hamantaschen* means "Haman's pockets," symbolizing the money Haman promised Ahasuerus in exchange for destroying the Jewish race. In Israel these pastries are called *oznei Haman* (Hebrew for "Haman's ears").

Hamantaschen

1½ tsp. baking powder

¾ tsp. kosher salt

4 c. all-purpose flour, plus more for dusting

1 c. (2 sticks) unsalted butter, room temperature

1 c. sugar

3 large eggs, divided

1½ c. jam or preserves

1. Whisk baking powder, salt, and 4 c. flour in a medium bowl. Beat butter and sugar in a large bowl until pale and fluffy, about 5 minutes. Add 2 eggs and beat again.

2. Gradually add dry ingredients; mix until dough comes together. Divide dough in half and form into two ¾-inch-thick disks. Cover and chill at least 2 hours.

3. Preheat to 350°. Let 1 disk of dough sit at room temperature until softened slightly, about 30 minutes.

4. Roll out dough on a lightly floured surface to about ¼ inch thick, dusting with flour as needed (use as little flour as possible). Cut out 3½-inch rounds with cutter and transfer to 2 parchment-lined baking sheets. Gather up scraps, reroll, and cut out additional rounds.

5. Lightly beat remaining egg in a small bowl to blend. Working a few at a time, brush edge of rounds with egg, then place 1½ tsp. filling in center. Fold sides up to make a triangle, pinching points gently to seal and leaving about 1 inch of filling exposed.

6. Brush sides of folded dough with beaten egg. Bake cookies, rotating baking sheets halfway through, until bottoms are golden brown, 18–22 minutes. Let cool on baking sheets. Repeat with other disk of dough. Makes about 24 servings.

Recipe adapted from bonappetit.com[5]

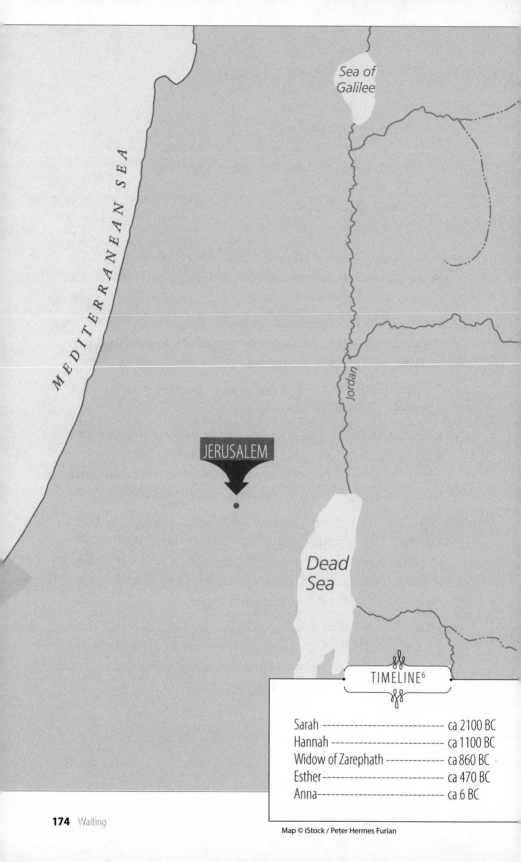

Sea of
Galilee

MEDITERRANEAN SEA

Jordan

JERUSALEM

Dead
Sea

TIMELINE⁶

Sarah ---------------------------- ca 2100 BC
Hannah ------------------------- ca 1100 BC
Widow of Zarephath ------------ ca 860 BC
Esther---------------------------- ca 470 BC
Anna----------------------------- ca 6 BC

Anna

Level 1: Reflect on the Reading

1. What kind of books do you like to read? Share a bit about your favorite kinds of stories or nonfiction books.

2. What did you learn about the setting of Anna's story in first-century Palestine?

3. If you were to grade Anna's waiting report card, what grade would you give her? What comments might you write on the report card?

4. Do you agree that an excellent story needs an element of suspense? How can that analogy help you as you live out the current chapter of your life?

5. What was the most important thing you learned about waiting well in chapter 5?

Read Anna's story in the context of the presentation of the baby Jesus: Luke 2:22–38.

1. Compare Simeon and Anna.

    a. How are Simeon and Anna alike?

    b. What is similar about their reactions to the baby Jesus?

    c. How do their reactions differ?

    d. If you had been in the temple court that day and heard Simeon's or Anna's words, what would have been your response?

2. Now concentrate on Anna.

    a. What facts about Anna do you discover in verses 36–38?

    b. With those facts in mind, write down three or four character qualities that describe Anna.

    c. Which of these characteristics would you like to see more of in your own life?

    d. What might you do to develop that characteristic?

3. Why do you think God included the story of Anna in His Word?

4. When you meet her in heaven, what might Anna tell you about those decades Scripture glosses over?

Level 3: Apply Anna's Story to Your Life

1. Anna's life probably changed dramatically after her husband died.

   a. How does her story demonstrate that even when we have experienced loss, God still has a purpose for our lives?

   b. Read the following verses and write what you learn about God's purpose for our lives.

   ☐ Psalm 57:2
   ☐ Proverbs 19:21
   ☐ Jeremiah 29:11
   ☐ Romans 8:28
   ☐ Ephesians 2:10

   c. Which verse is most meaningful to you? Make an artistic rendering of it in the margin of your Bible or write it on a 3 × 5 card to carry with you.

2. We may not recognize our purpose in life because we have preconceived expectations of what that purpose should look like.

   a. Read Isaiah 55:8–9 and Ephesians 3:20–21. Choose one of the passages and spend a few minutes meditating on it. Ask yourself questions like these: What words resonate with my soul? What is my response to this passage? Thanksgiving? Contrition? Joy? Peace? How does this passage relate to my life?

   b. Write down anything you want to remember from this time of meditation.

3. God chose to reveal the fact that the Messiah had come in the form of a baby to a poor, elderly woman. Probably few people even noticed Anna. Yet we know that God valued her.

   a. At times, we may feel worthless, invisible. That's when we need to turn to God's Word to learn our true worth. Read the following verses and write about our worth in God's eyes.

   ☐ Isaiah 43:4
   ☐ Luke 12:6–7
   ☐ 1 John 3:1

   b. Personalize one of these verses by inserting your name in place of the pronouns. (E.g., Because Sharla is precious and honored in My eyes . . .)

   c. How did personalizing the verse change your perception of it?

Level 4: Complete a Project

1. Anna and the rest of Israel were "waiting for the redemption of Jerusalem" (Luke 2:38). But while she was waiting, she was busy worshiping and praying. Take a few moments to think about what you can do while you are in a waiting season. Make an acrostic out of the word *WAIT*, writing down actions that begin with each letter (e.g., **W**orship, **A**bide, **I**nquire, **T**hank).

W

A

I

T

2. Do an Internet search of "images of Anna the prophetess." Which paintings or pictures resonate with your image of Anna? Are there any that contradict what we know about Anna from Scripture? Consider printing your favorite image (or saving it to your phone) to share with your group.

3. Imagine your life as a suspense-filled story. In the Table of Contents below, write out a title for each chapter of your life (e.g., "Growing Up in Gainesville," "Looking for Mr. Right," "Diapers and Sleep Deprivation"). In the next column, write down the element of suspense in that chapter—what were you waiting for? (To get out of Gainesville? For a godly husband? For a friend?) In the last column, reflect on the purpose you now see in the pause—what lessons did you learn? (Patience? The importance of character? To count your blessings?)

The Life Story of _____

Table of Contents

Chapter	Element of Suspense	Purpose in the Pause

Share a chapter of your story with your study group or with a friend. Be sure to include how you now see God's work in your life.

4. This week, remind yourself that God has a purpose in the pause by using your waiting times for good: take a book of devotions along to read in the doctor's waiting room, recite a favorite Bible verse while sitting at a stoplight, say a word of encouragement to someone waiting with you in the slowest grocery checkout lane. How did this activity change your view of waiting?

5. Reflect on the world's long wait for a Savior while listening to and meditating on Advent songs like the hymn "Come, Thou Long-Expected Jesus" or Chris Tomlin's "Emmanuel (Hallowed Manger Ground)."

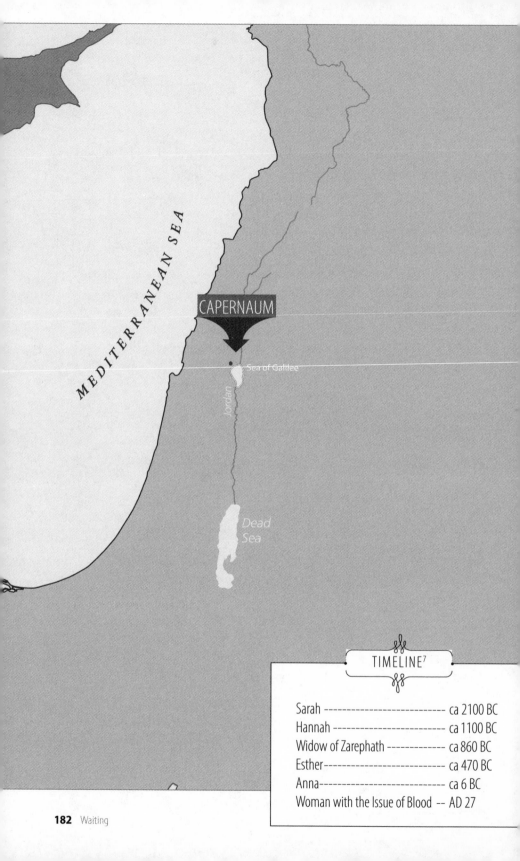

MEDITERRANEAN SEA

CAPERNAUM

Jordan

Sea of Galilee

Dead
Sea

TIMELINE[7]

Sarah ------------------------ ca 2100 BC
Hannah ----------------------- ca 1100 BC
Widow of Zarephath ------------ ca 860 BC
Esther------------------------ ca 470 BC
Anna-------------------------- ca 6 BC
Woman with the Issue of Blood -- AD 27

The Woman with the Issue of Blood
STUDY QUESTIONS

Level 1: Reflect on the Reading

1. What is the first word that comes to mind when you think of a doctor's waiting room? Why that word?

2. What did you learn about Capernaum and Jesus' ministry there that you didn't know before?

3. Have you ever suffered from a prolonged illness? Describe that time of your life: the illness or injury, how it changed your life, what you did to become well again.

4. If you were to grade the waiting report card for the bleeding woman, what grade would you give her? What comments might you add?

5. What was the most important thing you learned about waiting well in this chapter?

1. The account of the woman with an issue of blood is found in three of the Gospels. Read Matthew 9:20–22; Mark 5:25–34; and Luke 8:43–48.

   a. Matthew's account gives the basic elements of the story. Mark and Luke both add details that Matthew doesn't include. Write what you discover about her story in each of the Gospels.

Elements of the story in Matthew	Details Mark adds	Details Luke adds

   b. Pick one of the details that Mark or Luke adds and write how that detail enhanced your understanding of the account or how it changed your reaction to the story.

2. What characteristics of Jesus do you see in His interaction with the woman? Which of these characteristics most draws you to Jesus?

3. Write three or four words that describe the bleeding woman. Which of these characteristics do you want to emulate?

4. How does this real-life story of a suffering woman give you confidence to approach Jesus for help?

5. The bleeding woman spent twelve years and all of her money looking for healing. Often I spend a lot of time and money looking for answers from experts, and I forget to go to Jesus. What is your experience when you are in a waiting place? Do you go straight to Jesus? Or do you look in a lot of other places first? If you can, describe a specific incident of waiting and searching for answers.

6. The account of the suffering woman is a story within a story. Read Mark 5:21–43.

   a. What insights do you see about Veronica's story when you read it in the context of the account of Jairus and his daughter?

   b. How do you think Jairus was affected by Jesus' interaction with the bleeding woman?

   c. Picture yourself in the story. Do you see yourself as the important daughter or the lowly daughter? How does Jesus' interaction with that daughter influence your perception of how He sees you?

1. Many people bumped into Jesus that day in the crowd, but only the woman who reached out to touch the tassel on His clothing received healing.

   a. What was the difference?

   b. Why is faith necessary to receive Christ's gifts?

   c. Right now, are you more like one of the people in the crowd who casually bumped into Jesus, or are you like the woman who pushed through the mass of people to purposefully reach Him?

   d. Write a prayer asking the Holy Spirit to give you the strength and the faith to draw close to Jesus.

2. Jesus told the bleeding woman, "Go in peace" (Mark 5:34). The Greek word for peace is *eirene,* which means "the tranquil state of a soul assured of its salvation through Christ, and so fearing nothing from God and content with its earthly lot, of whatsoever sort that is."[2] The equivalent Old Testament word was *shalom,* which means "wholeness."

   a. In light of those definitions, why do you think Jesus added, "Go in peace" to His words of blessings to the bleeding woman, who was already healed?

   b. In the chapter we read, "Often when I am waiting, I am focused on getting what I want in the here and now. . . . But Jesus is more interested in eternal results." How have you experienced this in your own life?

3. If you have drawn near to Jesus for healing but haven't yet received it, how do you respond to this story? What emotions bubble up? What comfort or encouragement can you find?

Level 4: Complete a Project

1. Lamentations 3:25 encourages us to wait for God alone—apart from His gifts: "The LORD is good to those who wait for Him, to the soul who seeks Him." Look up Lamentations 3:22–26 to read the verse in context.

   a. Jot down three things you learned about God in this passage that inspire you to wait for Him.

   b. Verse 24 says, "The LORD is my portion." Other versions translate this phrase as "The LORD is my inheritance" or "The LORD is mine." Quietly consider these phrases for a moment. What is your reaction to these words?

   c. Write Lamentations 3:25 on a sticky note or card and post it where you are able to see it often this week.

2. The suffering woman reached out to touch the tassel on Jesus' garment. God instructed His people to wear these tassels to remind them of His commandments. Do an Internet search of "Jewish tassels" to find out more about them. Consider making one of these tassels (following online instructions) to remind you not only to follow God's commandments but to draw near to Jesus.

3. Try your hand at Bible journaling. In the margins of Mark 5 in your Bible, write down three insights you gained from your study of the story of the suffering woman. Or write, "Daughter, your faith has made you well; go in peace" (v. 34) in fancy lettering, making words that are especially meaningful to you larger than the others. Add color with colored pencils.

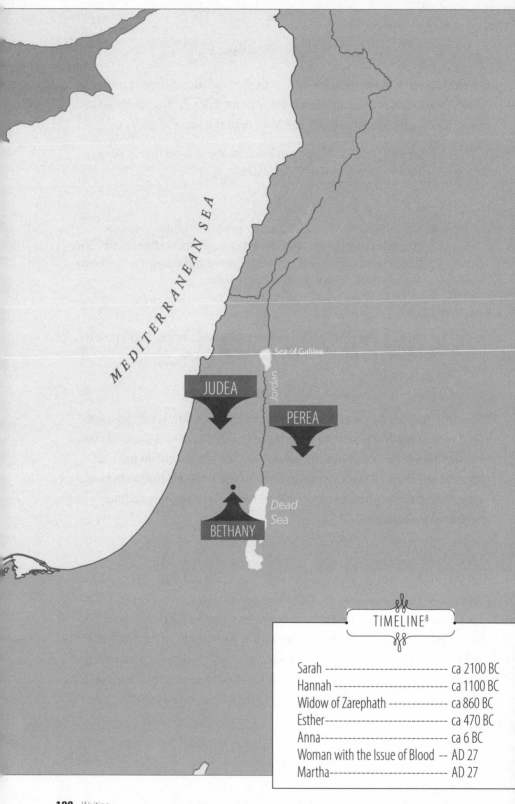

MEDITERRANEAN SEA

Sea of Galilee

JUDEA

Jordan

PEREA

Dead
Sea

BETHANY

TIMELINE[8]

Sarah --------------------------- ca 2100 BC
Hannah ------------------------- ca 1100 BC
Widow of Zarephath ------------ ca 860 BC
Esther--------------------------- ca 470 BC
Anna---------------------------- ca 6 BC
Woman with the Issue of Blood -- AD 27
Martha------------------------- AD 27

Martha

Level 1: Reflect on the Reading

1. Do you have a favorite recipe that requires a lot of time? What is it?

2. What did you learn about Martha and the resurrection of her brother that you didn't know before?

3. If you were to grade Martha's waiting report card, what grade would you give her? What comments might you write on the report card?

4. What was the most important thing you learned about waiting well from Martha's story?

Level 2: Dig into Scripture

1. Read about Martha in Luke 10:38–42 and John 11:1–44. What do you see about Martha—and yourself—in these accounts?

	Luke 10:38–42	John 11:1–44
Positive characteristics of Martha		
Negative characteristics of Martha		
Characteristics I see in myself in this story of Martha		

2. Now focus on John 11.

    a. How did Jesus interact with Martha?

    b. How did Jesus interact with Mary?

    c. What does this tell you about Jesus?

3. John 11 uses two different Greek words for love. Look up the following verses and write down what you discover about each type of love.

    a. *phileo*—"brotherly love"
        Matthew 10:37
        John 15:19
        Titus 3:15

    b. *agapo*—"to love dearly"
        John 10:17
        Hebrews 12:6
        1 John 4:10

    c. How does *agapao* love explain Jesus' long delay in coming to Martha and Mary?

    d. How could remembering Jesus' *agapao* love for you help you in times of delay?

4. Take a few minutes to meditate on John 11:1–44. Put yourself in the story and imagine yourself as Martha. Then answer these questions.

      a. What would you have been feeling during the four days of waiting?

      b. If you had spoken the words "Lord, if You had been here, my brother would not have died," what would have been the underlying emotions of that statement? Anger? Disappointment? Simple statement of facts?

      c. Jesus said: "I am the resurrection and the life. Whoever believes in Me, though he die, yet shall he live, and everyone who lives and believes in Me shall never die. Do you believe this?" (John 11:25–26). How would you have answered Jesus' question?

      d. What would have been your reaction to Jesus' tears?

Level 3: Apply Martha's Story to Your Own Life

1. What is your response to this statement: "Jesus loves us enough to use delay to answer our prayers in a bigger way than we can imagine"?

2. One of the reasons Jesus waited to come to Mary and Martha was to grow not only *their* faith but the faith of the disciples and the Jews who came to mourn. When has watching the faith of other Christians going through grief or hardship strengthened your own trust?

3. Picture your life as a recipe.

   a. Think about ingredients in your life during a difficult time in the past. Was there physical pain? hurt from other people? disappointment? List a few.

   b. Now think about how God worked through that struggle. Do you see how He used time to work out something bigger than you imagined?

   c. Next, list some ingredients of your current life that are confusing or disappointing. Add the word *time* to the bottom of the list.

   d. Are you willing to give God the time to create something beautiful out of these unclear elements? If so, write a prayer telling Him so.

Level 4: Complete a Project

1. If you are doing this study with a group, consider doing a tasting experiment. Bake your favorite cake recipe or cake mix before your group meets. Then, on the day of the meeting, set out a tray containing all the ingredients. Invite participants to taste the individual ingredients (except the raw egg, of course). Then offer some of the finished cake. Discuss how awful-tasting individual ingredients can become something delicious with a little time.

2. Use music to help you as you wait. Read or sing the words of the hymns "From Depths of Woe I Cry to Thee" and "Christ Be My Leader." Or find these songs on waiting on YouTube: "While I'm Waiting" by John Waller and "Waiting Here for You" by Christy Nockels.

3. Use a concordance or online Bible to look up verses on waiting. Choose one or two to post in prominent places around your home.

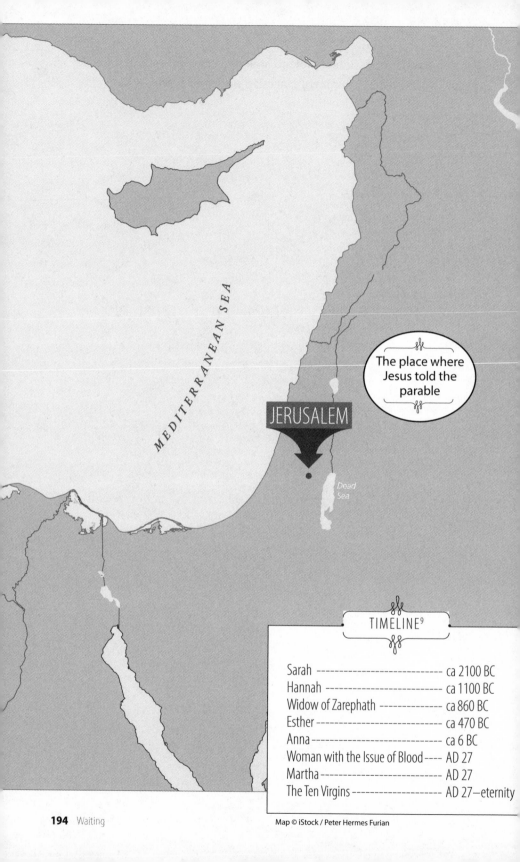

MEDITERRANEAN SEA

The place where Jesus told the parable

JERUSALEM

Dead Sea

Map © iStock / Peter Hermes Furian

The Ten Virgins

Level 1: Reflect on the Reading

1. What Advent activities do you do to help you wait for December 25?

2. If you were to grade the wise virgins' waiting report cards, what grade would you give them? What comments might you add?

3. How would you grade the foolish virgins? What would you want to tell them?

4. What was the most important thing you learned about waiting well from the ten virgins?

Level 2: Dig into Scripture

1. Read the parable of the ten virgins in Matthew 25:1–13.

    a. Jesus called five of the women foolish. Why were they foolish (v. 3)?

b. Why might the "foolish" virgins have neglected to bring extra oil?

c. Remember that the oil in the story represents God's grace that fuels our faith. (The Means of Grace include the Gospel, Baptism, and the Lord's Supper.) In our modern-day life, how do we sometimes neglect to refill our oil?

d. Jesus called five of the women wise. Why were they wise?

e. Jesus reminds us that our wait may be long and that we can't do it alone. We need a constant supply of the oil of grace. Make a list of practical ways to go to God—the source of grace. If you are doing this study in a group, share your ideas. Pick one of these activities to do this week. Then write out the list and keep it in your Bible so if your faith sputters, you have some practical ways to return to the Source.

I have made a few suggestions; add your own ideas below.

- Block out a morning or afternoon for a personal retreat. Spend time reading Scripture and journaling God's words to you.

- Write a prayer asking the Holy Spirit to give you fuel for your faith. Keep a copy of this prayer in your wallet or by your sink.

- Set a timer to go off at several times during the day. When it rings, pray the simple prayer, "Give ear, O Lord, to my prayer; listen to my plea for grace" (Psalm 86:6).

- Participate in the Lord's Supper, receiving Christ's grace through His body and blood.

-

-

-

-

f. The wise virgins could not share their oil; they could only direct the other women where to get some. How can we point people in our lives to the Source of oil?

g. Prayerfully read the story once more. Ask the Holy Spirit to show you where you are in the story. Write a prayer asking the Spirit to help you wait well.

2. Read Ephesians 5:22–33, a beautiful passage comparing marriage to Christ's relationship with us—the Church.

a. According to this passage, what are some ways marriage is like our relationship with Christ?

b. How does Paul describe Jesus as the perfect Bridegroom here?

c. Verse 24 says "the church submits to Christ." How is submitting like waiting?

3. Store up God's love in your heart as fuel for your faith. Look up these verses. Choose one to write on several sticky notes. Place them where you will see them often during the day.

   a. Psalm 86:15
   b. Zephaniah 3:17
   c. Ephesians 2:4–5
   d. 1 John 3:1
   e. 1 John 4:9

Level 3: Apply the Parable of the Ten Virgins to Your Life

1. The parable of the ten virgins revolves around Jewish wedding practices.

   a. What new insights did you gain about weddings in ancient Israel? (You might want to reread the information on page 132.)

   b. How do these insights relate to our wait for Christ to return?

   c. How does thinking of yourself as the Bride of Christ change your attitude toward waiting for the Bridegroom?

2. Read Jude 1:20–21 again.

   a. Review the "Waiting for Mercy" section of chapter 8. What are five things Jude encourages us to do?

      1.

      2.

      3.

      4.

      5.

b. Ask the Holy Spirit to show you which of these things you need to concentrate on this week. Write the answer here:

_____.

c. Think of a practical way you can focus on this action in the next seven days. (For example, if I wanted to concentrate on remembering myself as the Lord's beloved, I could memorize two or three of the Scriptures about God's love from "Dig into Scripture Question 3." Whenever Satan tries to whisper his lies, I would repeat these verses.)

Level 4: Complete a Project

1. Try making some simple oil candles with empty jars, water, vegetable oil, and large floating wicks (search for "large floating wicks" online). Fill a jar almost full with water and pour a little oil on top of the water. For the wick, insert one of the waxed wicks halfway through the center hole on the disc, and put it on top of the oil. Consider making two candles to burn during your study session, one with 1 tsp. of oil to represent the foolish virgins, and one with 2 tsp. of oil to symbolize the wise virgins.

2. End your study of waiting by reviewing all you have learned. Start by completing this chart, asking the Lord to remind you of the important lessons of His Word.
   (If you are doing this study in a group, you may want to take an extra week to discuss questions 2 and 3.)

Lady-in-Waiting	What she waited for	Most important lesson I learned from her life
Sarah		
Hannah		
Widow of Zarephath		
Esther		
Anna		
Woman with Issue of Blood		
Martha		
Wise Virgins		

3. Next, consider how this study has impacted your life by answering these questions:

    a. To which of the ladies-in-waiting did you most strongly relate?

    b. How have you changed through this study?

    c. What lesson about waiting well do you want to carry with you as you move through life?

Parting Thoughts

We are all waiting. Some of us may be waiting for meaningful work or for healed relationships. Others of us may be waiting for God to fix our finances or our health. But whatever else we may be waiting for, we are all waiting for Jesus. Whether we realize it or not, every one of us needs a Savior from our sins. Fortunately, God loved us so much that He sent His Son into the world to save us. He outlined His wonderful plan of salvation in His Word:

"For all have sinned and fall short of the glory of God" (Romans 3:23). No one is perfect. Everyone fails to meet God's standard of sinlessness. From the moment of the fall in the Garden of Eden, sin has prevented us from coming to Him and from entering heaven.

"For God so loved the world, that He gave His only Son, that whoever believes in Him should not perish but have eternal life" (John 3:16). God loved us so much that He sent His own Son to take the punishment we deserved for our sins and mistakes. Jesus' death enables us to live with God—forever.

"For by grace you have been saved through faith. And this is not your own doing; it is the gift of God" (Ephesians 2:8). God gives us faith to believe in Jesus. His grace and mercy save us from death.

"But to all who did receive Him, who believed in His name, He gave the right to become children of God" (John 1:12). By receiving Jesus in the waters of Baptism and the Holy Word of God, we become part of God's family.

I invite you to pray this prayer to the God who loves you and wants you to be part of His family:

> Father in heaven, I realize that I am a sinner and fall short of what You want for my life. I know that I cannot save myself or earn eternal life. Thank You for sending Your Son, Jesus, to die for me. Through the power of His resurrection, You have made me alive eternally. Help me to turn from my sins and follow You. Thank You that although I may still fail, You will forgive me because Jesus paid the price for my sins. Thank You for Your gift of faith in Jesus, my Savior, and for the promise of eternal life with You. In Jesus' name I pray. Amen.

God speaks His words of love and grace to you. Through God's free gift of faith in Jesus, you are part of God's family!

Acknowledgments

Life is filled with waiting. And writing is no different. In fact, writing and waiting seem to go hand in hand. Writers wait for an idea, wait for the right words, and wait for an editor to say yes. Even after the initial manuscript is finished, we writers wait for feedback, wait to see a cover design, and wait for the book to be released.

I could not have endured all this waiting without God and the significant people in my life who supported me. I wish to thank:

God: Through the months of writing this book, You helped me see that waiting is not a punishment nor a waste of time. Every moment of waiting has been an opportunity for me to lean on You.

John: Thank you for so patiently waiting for me when I have spent hours glued to my computer. Without your love and support, this book would never have been written.

Family: Anna, Nate, Aaron, Andrew, Alexander, Abigail, Nathaniel, and Mary—although I can barely wait to see you, I know the wait is worth it. Thank you for your love.

Writing friends: Thanks to Lara Krupicka, Jan May, Suzanne Reeves, Kim Gunderson, Julie Jung-Kim, Julie Kloster, Terri Krauss, Linda MacKillop, Catherine McNiel, Shelli Massie, Shayne Moore, Margaret Philbrick, JoHannah Reardon, Afton Rorvik, Aubrey Sampson, and Shelly Wildman. You all know the waiting life of a writer firsthand. Thank you for your companionship in this journey and for your wisdom in shaping this book.

Bible study gals: Pam Barrett, Rhonda McIntyre, Deb Morris, and Sue Scholtz—how can I thank you enough for test-driving this study and for walking with me through the waiting times of life? Thank you for the gift of laughter!

Church family: Thanks to the people of Hope Lutheran who waited with us through the months of John's treatment.

Concordia Publishing House: Thanks especially to Peggy Kuethe whose skillful editing made *Waiting* a better book. Your wisdom and friendship are invaluable. Thanks to the rest of the CPH staff who have all worked to bring the book to the many ladies-in-waiting across the country.

Study Guide Answers

Level 1: Reflect on the Reading: 1. Answers will vary. 2. Answers will vary. 3. Answers will vary. 4. God revealed He was the one in control by directing the course of their life from Ur to Haran to Canaan. He revealed Himself to Abraham with a new name, *El-Shaddai*, or "Lord Almighty." 5. Answers will vary.

Level 2: Dig into Scripture: 1. a. Both talk about how Sarah willingly goes with Abraham, obeying him. b. Submission and obedience to Abraham and to the Lord. c. The Lord promises Abram He will make him into a great nation. He will bless him and make his name great. 2. a. God promises Abram his offspring will be as numerous as the stars. b. Sarah is not mentioned. c. He instructs Abram to cut up animals and splay the pieces out. God's presence, in the form of a flaming torch and a smoking fire pot, passes between the pieces. 3. a. Sarai is self-centered, determined to have her way, manipulative. b. Perhaps Abram thought this was what Sarai wanted and he wanted to make her happy. Perhaps he realized God had not mentioned Sarai in the promises. c. The plan backfired because once Hagar became pregnant, she despised Sarai. The baby was not going to be considered Sarai's. 4. Now God promises Abraham will have a child through Sarah. 5. a. The promise is the same. b. He repeated it for Sarah's benefit. c. Sarah's laughter reveals she doubts God's promise. d. This passage shows she is obedient to Abraham, who tells her to make some bread. Perhaps it also shows she is curious—she listens in on the conversation. Her lying may show that she was not always honest or that she was fearful. 6. a. Here Sarah laughs out of joy, not out of doubt. b. Sarah is joyful and thankful. 7. Sarah's predominant character quality is faith. 8. Genesis 12:1–9 and 1 Peter 3:5–6: submissive and obedient; Genesis 16: self-centered, focused on having her own way, manipulative; Genesis 18:1–15: doubting, obedient to Abraham, curious, lying may show she is dishonest or fearful; Genesis 21:1–7: joyful and thankful; Hebrews 11:11 strong faith. 9. a. God wanted Abraham to trust Him and trust means believing even when the whole picture is not revealed. b. God did not reveal Abram's final destination. Abram had to trust God step-by-step. c. Answers will vary but perhaps will include a reassurance that God often reveals His will one step at a time. He gives the knowledge and guidance we need for now and asks us to trust Him for the next step at the right time.

Level 3: Apply Sarah's Story to Your Life: Answers will vary.

Level 4: Complete a Project: Answers will vary.

Chapter 2

Level 1: Reflect on the Reading: 1. Answers will vary. 2. Answers will vary. 3. Answers will vary. 4. Both Sarah and Hannah waited years to have a child. Both watched their husbands have a child with another woman. Sarah did not wait patiently but tried to change the situation with her own plans, which backfired on her. She laughed when God told her she would have a child within a year. Hannah, on the other hand, took her desires to God and surrendered them into His care. She exhibited a great trust in God. Although we do not see Sarah trusting God in Genesis, she is later commended for great faith in Hebrews 11. 5. Answers will vary.

Level 2: Dig into Scripture: 1. a. An *inclusio* is a section of text formed by the use of the same word or phrase both at the beginning and the end. This word highlights the meaning of the section. b. The Hebrew word for sacrifice: *zabach*. c. 1 Samuel 1:11: "O LORD of hosts, if You will indeed look on the affliction of Your servant and remember me and not forget Your servant, but will give to Your servant a son, then I will give him to the LORD all the days of his life, and no razor shall touch his head." 1 Samuel 1:28: "Therefore I have lent him to the LORD. As long as he lives, he is lent to the LORD." d. The Israelites were sacrificing animals and grain from their farms, but Hannah was sacrificing her own child. The Israelites were sacrificing from their abundance—they had other animals and more grain. But Hannah was sacrificing her only child. She didn't know if God would give her another. e. Answers will vary, but communal sacrifices might include monetary offerings, the sacrifice of time to worship, the sacrifice of thanksgiving and praise. 2. a. A sacrifice of trust in the Lord. b. A sacrifice of thanksgiving. c. A sacrifice of a broken and contrite heart. d. A sacrifice of prayer. e. Answers will vary. 3. a. Hannah addresses her prayer to the Lord of hosts, which demonstrates her acknowledgment of God's sovereign rule over creation and her life. b. Hannah is humble; she is honest about her sadness; she relinquishes her desires to God. 4. a. Sorrow, sadness, bitterness of soul. b. She is no longer sad. c. She had surrendered her petition and desire to the God who was able to change her situation. She had peace because she trusted God. d. Answers will vary. 5. a. Hannah rejoices in the Lord. b. It is significant because she had just left her child to live in the tabernacle—away from her. Normal emotions would be sadness and grief, but she finds joy in the Lord and not in her circumstances.

Level 3: Apply Hannah's Story to Your Life: 1. Answers will vary. 2. Answers will vary but might include sending an encouraging email, asking a friend out to lunch. 3. Answers will vary.

Level 4: Complete a Project: 1. Answers will vary. 2. Answers will vary. 3. Hannah talks about God's holiness, His uniqueness, His strength (1 Samuel 2:2). She praises His omnipotence and judgment (v. 3). She mentions His ability to bring death or life, poverty or wealth, humility or fame (vv. 6–7). She praises His power in creation (v. 8).

Chapter 3

Level 1: Reflect on the Reading: Answers will vary.

Level 2: Dig into Scripture: 1. a. God tells Elijah to tell King Ahab there will be no rain for the next few years. Then God instructs Elijah to hide at the brook Cherith, where ravens will bring food for him. It sets the scene for the widow's story because it tells us why there is no food. b. During the time of Elijah, the people of Israel were worshiping false gods, including Baal. Elijah's very name gave testimony to the true God, Yahweh. c. Ravens are usually scavengers, eating scraps of food instead of providing food. Ravens are unclean animals, yet God used them for His purpose. d. Answers will vary. 2. a. Zarephath was a suburb of Sidon, Queen Jezebel's hometown and a center of Baal worship. b. Answers will vary. c.

Passage	What God Provided	How Often God Provided
1 Kings 17:15–16	Flour and oil	Daily
Exodus 16:15–21, 31	Manna	Daily (except on the Sabbath)
Matthew 6:11	Bread	Daily

d. God wants us to rely on Him every day. Often when our freezers and bank accounts are full, we take His provision for granted. e. Answers will vary. f. The Word of the Lord was "Go at once to Zarephath of Sidon and stay there." Elijah obeyed. g. The Word of the Lord comes to us through Scripture.

3. a.

Person	Response to Tragedy
Widow	She thinks the tragedy is because of her sin.
Elijah	He prays to God.
Me	Answers will vary.

3. b. From Elijah's response, we can learn the best thing to do in any crisis is to take the problem to God. We don't have to understand why the problem is happening, only that God sees what is going on and that He promises to work everything to our good.

Level 3: Apply the Widow's Story to Your Life 1. Answers will vary. 2. Deuteronomy 31:8—f, Isaiah 26:3—e, Isaiah 58:11—a, Jeremiah 31:3—d, Micah 7:18–19—g, Matthew 6:31–33—b, 2 Corinthians 1:3–4—c, James 1:5—h. 3. Answers will vary. 4. Answers will vary. 5. Answers will vary.

Level 4: Complete a Project: Answers will vary.

Chapter 4

Level 1: Reflect on the Reading: Answers will vary.

Level 2: Dig into Scripture: 1. a. She might have been happy because royal life was luxurious or because it was an honor to be chosen. But she might have been unhappy because she had to leave her family and friends. She had to abandon her Jewish customs and any hope for a "normal" life. b. Perhaps she exhibited humility, kindness, and respect. c. Answers will vary. 2. a. "And who knows whether you have not come to the kingdom for such a time as this?" b. He is saying that perhaps God placed her in the position of queen so that she could save the Jews. c. Answers will vary. d. Relief and deliverance will come from another place, but she will perish. e. Because God is giving us an opportunity to be a part of His plan. We are His agents in the world. Also, obedience is a way to demonstrate our love for God (John 14:15). f. She fasted for three days and asked all the Jews to fast with her. g. When we are faced with a great task or important decision, we need to take a step back and prepare by waiting and praying instead of rushing ahead. 3. Answers will vary. 4. a. The king couldn't sleep; he asked for the book of records, and the attendant read about Mordecai exposing the assassination plot. Haman had come to ask about hanging Mordecai, and the king asks *him* to honor Mordecai. b. Answers will vary but might include the following: God is at work for us, working everything out for our good even when we can't do anything for ourselves. 5. a. She is humble and polite but still bold. b. She lets Hegai decide what she should wear when she goes to the king. She humbles herself to fast for three days before approaching the king. c. Answers will vary but might include the following: Humility helps us remember God is the ruler of the universe and we are not. Humility enables us to be receptive to what God is doing in our lives.

Level 3: Apply Esther's Story to Your Life: 1. Answers will vary. 2. Roadblocks could prevent us from making poor choices or could force us to slow down long enough to go to the Lord. 3. a. Courage in waiting looks like confidence that God will take care of me. It doesn't whine or worry. It prays and rests in God's love. It is courage to trust God, giving up my own agenda. b. Answers will vary.

Level 4: Complete a Project: a. Chapter 1: Queen Vashti refuses to appear, making way for a new queen. Chapter 2: Esther is chosen to be queen. Mordecai discovers an assassination plot. Chapter 3: Haman casts the *pur* (the lot) to choose the date of the destruction of the Jews, a date almost twelve months ahead. Chapter 4: Mordecai tells Esther she may have been chosen to be queen in order to save her people. Chapter 5: The king extends the scepter to Esther. Haman builds a gallows for Mordecai. Chapter 6: The king can't sleep and reads about Mordecai exposing the murder plot. Haman happens to be in the palace that night. Chapter 7: Haman is hanged on the gallows he constructed for Mordecai. Chapter 8: Because the date chosen for the destruction of the Jews was nine months away, the news of the edict giving Jews the right to defend themselves had time to reach all the provinces of King Ahasuerus. Chapter 9: God gave the Jews the ability to defend themselves. Chapter 10: Mordecai, who could have been hanged by Haman, was made second in rank to King Ahasuerus. b. Answers will vary. 2. Answers will vary. 3. Recipe.

Chapter 5

Level 1: Reflect on the Reading: 1. Answers will vary. 2. The people of Israel were waiting for relief from foreign rulers, waiting for a prophet, waiting for a Savior. 3. Answers will vary. 4. Answers will vary. 5. Answers will vary.

Level 2: Dig into Scripture: 1. a. Simeon and Anna were both waiting for the Messiah. b. Both Anna and Simeon responded in thanksgiving for the Savior. c. Simeon praises God for letting him see the Messiah and declares his life complete. He warns Mary that her Son will cause the rising and falling of many in Israel and that a sword will pierce her soul. Anna immediately begins to tell others about the Savior. d. Answers will vary. 2. a. Anna was a prophetess. She was a widow and at least eighty-four years old. She spent her time in the temple worshiping, with fasting and prayer. She told others about the Messiah. b. Answers will vary but may include the following: faithful to God, patient, devoted in prayer, self-sacrificing (she worshiped with fasting), bold in her witness. c. Answers will vary. d. Answers will vary. 3. Answers will vary but may include the following: to show us that even when we experience loss and feel useless, that our lives have purpose right where we are and that we are of value to God. 4. Answers will vary but might include the following: Anna might share that although her life did not turn out as she had planned, her time in the temple was a great blessing, that she grew closer to the Lord and appreciated the chance to minister to other women who came to worship.

Level 3: Apply Anna's Story to Your Life: 1. a. Anna did not retreat from life when she became a widow; instead, she dedicated herself to God. God demonstrated her worth by allowing her to be one of the few people who recognized Jesus as Messiah. b. Psalm 57:2: God promises to fulfill His purpose for me. Proverbs 19:21: We may make plans, but it is the purpose of the Lord that will stand. Jeremiah 29:11: God has plans to give us a hope and a future. Romans 8:28: God works everything for the good of those who love Him. Ephesians 2:10: We are God's workmanship and He has prepared good works for us. c. Answers will vary. 2. Answers will vary. 3. a. Isaiah 43:4: We are precious and honored in God's sight. He loves us. Luke 12:6–7: Jesus tells us we are worth much more than sparrows and that God knows everything about us—even the number of hairs on our heads. 1 John 3:1: God's love for us is so great that He calls us His children. b. Answers will vary. c. Answers will vary.

Level 4: Complete a Project: 1. Answers will vary but might include the following: W—watch for God's action in your life, weed out sins and harmful attitudes, work where God has placed you; A—accept God's will, acknowledge His authority in your life, adore the Creator of the universe; I—intercede for others, increase your time in God's Word, identify things you can be grateful for; T—tell others about Jesus, talk with a trusted Christian friend, think on God's promises. 2. Answers will vary. 3. Answers will vary. 4. Answers will vary. 5. Answers will vary.

Chapter 6

Level 1: Reflect on the Reading: Answers will vary.

Level 2: Dig into Scripture: 1. a. Elements of the story in Matthew: The woman suffered from a discharge of blood for twelve years (v. 20). She came up behind Jesus and touched His garments (v. 20). She told herself that if she only touched His garment, she would be made well (v. 21). Jesus turned and told her, "Take heart, daughter; your faith has made you well" (v. 22). She was healed instantly (v. 22). Details Mark adds: The woman had suffered under many physicians and spent all she had on treatments (v. 26). She heard reports about Jesus (v. 27). Jesus perceived power had gone out from Him and asked, "Who touched Me?" (v. 30). The disciples pointed out that the crowd was pressing in around Him (v. 31). The woman came in fear and trembling and told Jesus the whole truth (v. 33). Jesus told her, "Go in peace" (v. 34). Details Luke adds: The woman had spent all her living on physicians (v. 43). Everyone denied touching Jesus (v. 45). The woman saw she was not hidden (v. 47). She declared in the presence of the people why she had touched Jesus and how she had been healed (v. 47). b. Answers will vary. 2. Answers will vary, but characteristics of Jesus might include caring, compassionate, desires truth, values faith, notices everyone. 3. Answers will vary, but words that describe the bleeding woman might include persistent, trusting, frightened, desperate, brave, faithful, honest. 4. Answers will vary. 5. Answers will vary. 6. a. Answers will vary but might include the following: A great crowd immediately gathered when Jesus arrived by boat. Veronica was just as helpless and just as loved by a life-giving Savior as Jairus's daughter. The theme of both stories is faith. Jairus was also desperate—his daughter was at the point of death. b. Answers will vary but might include the following:

Jairus may have been impatient as Jesus took time for someone else while his daughter was at death's door. But he might have been encouraged by the healing of the woman. c. Answers will vary.

Level 3: Apply the Suffering Woman's Story to Your Life: 1. a. The woman had faith in Jesus' power to heal. b. God doesn't force His gifts on anyone. We need a receptive attitude. Imagine someone offering you a gift. She is making it available to you, but it isn't yours until you open your hands and receive it. God gives us the faith to receive. c. Answers will vary. d. Answers will vary. 2. a. Perhaps Jesus wanted the woman to know that she had received an even more important blessing than healing of the body. Her soul had also been healed through faith. b. Answers will vary. 3. Answers will vary.

Level 4: Complete a Project: 1. a. Possible answers include: His love is steadfast, His mercies never come to an end, His mercies are new every morning, His faithfulness is great, God is good to those who wait for Him. b. Answers will vary. c. Answers will vary. 2. Project. 3. Project.

Chapter 7

Level 1: Reflect on the Reading: Answers will vary.

Level 2: Dig into Scripture: 1. Luke 10:38–42: Positive characteristics of Martha: willing to help, practiced hospitality. Negative characteristics of Martha: distracted with much serving, anxious, troubled. Characteristics I see in myself: Answers will vary. John 11:1–44: Positive characteristics of Martha: expressed strong faith in Jesus as Healer and as Messiah. Negative characteristics: She believed Jesus would raise Lazarus on the Last Day, but she seemed to doubt that He could raise him now. Characteristics I see in myself: Answers will vary. 2. a. Jesus had a conversation with Martha; He asked questions to draw out her faith. b. Jesus cried with Mary; He showed great empathy. c. Jesus meets each of us where we are. He knows our individual needs and cares for them. 3. a. Matthew 10:37: *Phileo* is a family love—how we love parents and children. John 15:19: *Phileo* is how the world loves its own—how we love people who are like us. Titus 3:15: *Phileo* is how we love our brothers and sisters in the faith. b. John 10:17: *Agapao* is how the Father loves the Son. Hebrews 12:6: *Agapao* is a love that is deep enough to discipline someone for their good. 1 John 4:10: It is the Father's love for us—a love strong enough to sacrifice His Son for us. c. *Agapao* love considers what is best for the person in the long run. Jesus knew raising Lazarus from the dead would be a bigger miracle than healing him. That act would strengthen Mary and Martha's faith and the faith of many others. d. Answers will vary but might include the following: If I remember that Jesus' love for me was deep enough that He would die for me, maybe I can trust that His love wants the best for me right now. 4. Answers will vary.

Level 3: Apply Martha's Story to Your Life: Answers will vary.

Level 4: Complete a Project: Answers will vary.

Chapter 8

Level 1: Reflect on the Reading: Answers will vary.

Level 2: Dig into Scripture: 1. a. They were foolish because they did not bring extra oil for their lamps. b. The foolish virgins might have neglected to bring extra oil because they didn't think the wait for the bridegroom would be long. Or perhaps they were too excited about the wedding to think ahead, or they were too busy preparing their clothes and appearance to plan for the practical matters of a long wait. c. Answers will vary but may include the following: We neglect going to church and participating in the Lord's Supper. We don't spend time in God's Word. We focus on difficulties in our lives and not on the fact that the Holy Spirit lives inside of us to strengthen us. d. The wise women brought extra oil along with the lamps. e. Other ideas might include: Listening to Christian music. Taking a walk outside and focusing on God's creation. Counting your blessings. Reminding yourself of God's love to you by reading 1 John 4:7–10. f. Answers will vary but might include the following: extending an invitation to church or Bible study, sending a card with an encouraging Bible verse, telling others the difference Christ has made in our lives. g. Answers will vary. 2. a. Christ is the Head of the Church; the husband is the head of the wife. The Church submits to Christ; wives submit to their husbands. Christ loved the Church and gave Himself up for her; husbands are to love their wives with the same sacrificial kind of love. b. Jesus loved His Bride so much that He gave Himself up for her. He cleanses and sanctifies the Bride so she is holy and without blemish. c. In both submitting and waiting, we give up our control of events and our own timetables. 3. Participants write out Bible verses on notes to post in their homes.

Level 3: Apply the Parable of the Ten Virgins to Your Life: 1. a. Answers will vary but may include the following: The couple were legally considered husband and wife at the betrothal, but they couldn't be together. The bridegroom came to get the bride. There was a grand procession to the house the groom had prepared for his wife. b. We belong to Christ now, even though we are still waiting for Him to come to get us. Jesus will come and take us to the home He has prepared for us. We will all celebrate the marriage of the Bridegroom and the Bride—the Church. c. Answers will vary. 2. a. 1. Remind yourself you are the beloved. 2. Build yourself up in the holy faith. 3. Pray in the Holy Spirit. 4. Keep yourself in the love of God. 5. Wait for the mercy of the Lord Jesus Christ. b. Answers will vary. c. Answers will vary.

Level 4: Complete a Project: 1. Crafting oil candles. 2. Answers will vary but may include the following:

Lady-in-Waiting	What she waited for	Characteristics of this woman I want to emulate	Most important lesson I learned from her life
Sarah	Waited for a child	Obedience to Abraham, her faith (as commended in Hebrews)	Answers will vary.
Hannah	Waited for a child	Willingness to sacrifice her desires, patience	
Widow of Zarephath	Waited for oil and flour	Willingness to share, waiting on God daily	
Esther	Waited a year to go to the king from the harem, then waited for courage and wisdom to approach the king	Smart, courageous, humble	
Anna	Waited for the Messiah	Patient, faithful, trusting, prayerful	
Woman with Issue of Blood	Waited for healing	Strong faith, boldness	
Martha	Waited for Jesus to come for Lazarus	Strong profession of faith	
Wise Virgins	Waited for the bridegroom to come	Thinking ahead, preparing for a long wait	

NOTES

Chapter 1

1. For a more detailed map, see *TLSB*, p. 33.
2. Howard S. Vos, *New Illustrated Manners and Customs: How the People of the Bible Really Lived* (Nashville, TN: Thomas Nelson, 1999), 6–18.
3. Edward A. Engelbrecht, ed. *Lutheran Bible Companion: Volume 1: Introduction and Old Testament* (St. Louis, MO: Concordia Publishing House, 2014), 49–50.
4. H. D. M. Spence and Joseph S. Exell, *The Pulpit Commentary Volume 1: Genesis Exodus* (Grand Rapids, MI: Wm. B. Eerdmans Publishing Co., 1950), 175.
5. Victor H. Matthews, *The Cultural World of the Bible: An Illustrated Guide to Manners and Customs* (Grand Rapids, MI: Baker Academic, 1988, 1991, 2006, 2015), 23–24.
6. Robert G. Hoerber, ed., *Concordia Self-Study Bible* (St. Louis, MO: Concordia Publishing House, 1986), 31. Used by permission.
7. Ibid., 30.

Chapter 2

1. For a more detailed map, see *TLSB* Color Map 1.
2. Edward A. Engelbrecht, ed., *Lutheran Bible Companion: Volume 1: Introduction and Old Testament* (St. Louis, MO: Concordia Publishing House, 2014), 230.
3. *TLSB*, p. 435.
4. "Shiloh," *Bible Hub*, biblehub.com/topical/s/shiloh.htm.
5. Robert G. Hoerber, ed., *Concordia Self-Study Bible* (St. Louis, MO: Concordia Publishing House, 1986], 123).
6. *TLSB*, p. 435.
7. Elizabeth Ahlman, *Ruth: More Than a Love Story* (St. Louis, MO: Concordia Publishing House, 2014), 15.
8. "Lexicon: Strong's H7592 sha'al," *Blue Letter Bible*, https://www.blueletterbible.org/lang/lexicon.cfm?Strongs=H7592&t=KJV.
9. Dictionary.com. http://dictionary.reference.com/browse/exult?s=t.

Chapter 3

1. For a more detailed map, see *TLSB* Color Map 1.
2. *TLSB*, p. 529.
3. *TLSB*, p. 1227.
4. Arthur W. Klinck and Erich H. Kiehl, *Everyday Life in Bible Times* (St. Louis, MO: Concordia Publishing House, 1947, 1969, 1995), 71.
5. Klinck and Kiehl, 92–93.
6. J. D. Douglas, ed., *The Illustrated Bible Dictionary: Part 3 Parable-Zuzim* (Wheaton, IL: Tyndale House Publishers, 1980), 1673.
7. *NIV Archaeological Study Bible* (Grand Rapids, MI: Zondervan, 2005), 514.
8. Andrew Murray, *Waiting on God* (Renaissance Classics, 2012), 65. Used by permission.

Chapter 4

1. For a more detailed map, see *TLSB*, p. 1396.
2. John F. Brug, *People's Bible Commentary: Ezra/Nehemiah/Esther* (St. Louis, MO: Concordia Publishing House, 2005) 14. Used by permission.
3. Ibid., 159.
4. *TLSB*, p. 763.
5. *TLSB*, p. 765.
6. James M. Freeman, *Manners and Customs in the Bible* (Plainfield, NJ: Logos International, 1972), 207.
7. *TLSB*, p. 768.

Chapter 5

1. For a more detailed map, see *TLSB* Color Map 4.
2. *TLSB*, p. 389.
3. John MacArthur, *Twelve Extraordinary Women: How God Shaped Women of the Bible and What He Wants to Do with You* (Nashville, TN: Thomas Nelson, 2005), 137. Used by permission.
4. *TLSB*, p. 1078.
5. *Luther's Small Catechism with Explanation* (St. Louis, MO: Concordia Publishing House, 1986, 1991), 59.

Chapter 6

1. For a more detailed map, see *TLSB*, Color Map 4.
2. The Bible does not give her condition a name, but most commentaries state that it was likely a uterine hemorrhage.
3. Joe M. Sprinkle, "Clean, Unclean," *Baker's Evangelical Dictionary of Biblical Theology,* 1996, http://www.biblestudytools.com/dictionaries/bakers-evangelical-dictionary/clean-unclean.html.
4. Frank Viola and Mary DeMuth, *The Day I Met Jesus: The Revealing Diaries of Five Women from the Gospels* (Grand Rapids, MI: Baker Books, 2015), Kindle edition 1496 of 2286. Used by permission.
5. *TLSB*, p. 1665.
6. Fred Rosner, "Julius Preuss and His Classic Biblisch-Talmudische Medizin," *Medicine in the Bible and Talmud,* (Hoboken, NJ: KTAV Publishing House, 1977), 32, as quoted on Google Books, https://books.google.com/books?id=SL34EWxAJfYC&pg=PA32&dg=vaginal+bleeding+Medicine+in+the+Bible+and+Talmud&hl=en&sa=X&ved=0ahUKEwi6-K2z5ZbNAhUGGIIKHR7PC9sQ6AEIMDAA#v=onepage&q=vaginal%20bleeding%20Medicine%20in%20the%20Bible%20and%20Talmud&f=false.
7. "Luke 8:43," *Cambridge Bible for Schools and Colleges,* as quoted on Bible Hub, http://bible-hub.com/commentaries/luke/8-43.htm.
8. *TLSB*, p. 1665.
9. "Lexicon: Strong's G2899 *kraspedon*," *Blue Letter Bible*, https://www.blueletterbible.org/lang/lexicon/lexicon.cfm?Strongs=G2899&t=KJV.).
10. "Lexicon: Strong's G4982 *sozo*," *Blue Letter Bible*, https://www.blueletterbible.org/lang/lexicon.cfm?Strongs=G4982&t=KJV.

11. Andrew Murray, *Waiting on God* (Renaissance Classics, 2012), 73. Used by permission.

Chapter 7

1. For a more detailed map, see *TLSB*, Color Map 4.
2. "Lexicon: Strong's G963 *Bethania*," *Blue Letter Bible*, https://www.blueletterbible.org/lang/lexicon/lexicon.cfm?Strongs=G963&t=KJV
3. "Bethany," *Bible Study Tools*, www.biblestudytools.com/dictionary/bethany.
4. *NIV Archaeological Study Bible* (Grand Rapids, MI: Zondervan, 2005), 1688.
5. "What does 'Christ' actually mean?" *Our Rabbi Jesus*. July 6, 2012. ourrabbijesus.com/articles/what-does-the-word-christ-actually-mean.
6. From *TLSB*, p. 1803.
7. Adapted from Deb Burma, *Living a Chocolate Life* (St. Louis, MO: Concordia Publishing House, 2015) 79–80. Used by permission.

Chapter 8

1. For a more detailed map, see *TLSB*, Color Map 4.
2. Paul E. Kretzmann, *Popular Commentary of the Bible: The New Testament Volume 1* [St. Louis, MO: Concordia Publishing House], 139
3. Robert G. Hoerber, ed., *Concordia Self-Study Bible* (St. Louis, MO: Concordia Publishing House, 1986), 1599.
4. Arthur W. Klinck and Erich H. Kiehl, *Everyday Life in Bible Times* (St. Louis, MO: Concordia Publishing House, 1947, 1969, 1995), 158–59.
5. Justin Holcomb, "What Is Advent?" *Christianity.com*, www.christianity.com/christian-life/christmas/what-is-advent.html.
6. C. S. Lewis, *Mere Christianity*, as quoted on Good Reads, http://www.goodreads.com/quotes/363092-if-i-find-in-myself-desires-which-nothing-in-this.

Study Guide

1. For a more detailed map, see *TLSB*, p. 33.
2. For a more detailed map, see *TLSB* Color Map 1.
3. Ibid.
4. For a more detailed map, see *TLSB*, p. 1396.
5. Recipe adapted from http://www.bonappetit.com/recipe/hamentaschen.
6. For a more detailed map, see *TLSB* Color Map 4.
7. Ibid.
8. Ibid.
9. Ibid.